Spooked

Spooked

Talking About the Supernatural

Edited by Tony Watkins

Authentic

www.DamarisBooks.com

Coverdesign by fourninezero design.
Typeset by GCS, Leighton Buzzard, Beds,
in 11 on 13 Palatino
Print management by Adare Carwin
Printed in the UK by J.H. Haynes & Co., Sparkford

Contents

Introduction to the *Talking About* Series

Have you ever had one of those conversations when you know you ought to be able to bring in a Christian perspective? The problem is how to do it. As the conversation goes on you become more and more anxious. You know you have a good opportunity to say something; you know you *should* say something – but you just can't think what. Probably all of us have been there at some time or other. Many of us would like a little help on thinking through some issues beforehand.

It seems to me that there are three areas of conversation which frequently cry out for a Christian angle to be included: personal issues in the lives of friends, family or work colleagues; big issues in society generally; and things in the media. They often overlap, of course. So when Nick Pollard was asked to contribute a regular column for *Idea,* the Evangelical Alliance's magazine for members,[1] it seemed a great opportunity to focus on some of the overlapping issues which people are talking about. The articles aim to help readers understand some of what is being said about these issues in today's world, and particularly to explore some of the underlying ideas. The primary aim, of course, is to help equip people for having more and more productive conversations with friends, colleagues and family. It soon became apparent that this is just the kind of help that many Christians feel they need.

So, this series of short books came to be. Each of the books takes the basic ingredients of what Nick has written in one of his articles and develops them into something more substantial, but still light and easily digested. Nick significantly develops his 800-word *Idea* article into the opening chapter of each book. Then come some extra ingredients: a biblical perspective on the issue; articles on key aspects of the central theme; study guides on relevant films, books or television programmes; and an introduction to one or more key thinkers whose work still influences our culture. Some of these chapters have been developed from material published on Damaris' CultureWatch website (www. culturewatch.org), others have been commissioned especially for this book. Finally, sprinkled throughout the mix are some great quotes which help to spice up your conversations about the issues we're examining (many of these quotes have come from another great Damaris resource, www.ToolsForTalks.com – a collection of tools for speakers whether they are teaching the Bible to Christians or engaged in evangelism).[2]

This is not the kind of book to sit down and read straight through. Instead it has been designed for dipping into. Each of the chapters stands independently of the others, though of course they're all linked by the common theme. One of the consequences of this is that you will, at times, find a little overlap between chapters. We've minimised this as much as we can without taking away anything essential from one or more of the chapters. The study guides are suitable for individual reflection or for use in home groups. If you do use them in a group setting, don't slavishly work through all the questions – we've given you more than enough so that you can select some that you feel are particularly helpful to your group. Finally, the last chapter, introducing an influential thinker, is inevitably harder going than earlier chapters – which is why it is at the end of the book. It is worth taking time to try to understand the line of argument and why it is significant, but the chapter is not essential for getting to grips with the central issue around which the book revolves.

We hope you will find this interesting, entertaining and stimulating. But our prayer is that this will enable you to be more effective in talking about the good news of Jesus Christ within today's world, whether – as Nick frequently says – you are talking from a pulpit or over the garden fence.

Tony Watkins

Notes

[1] For more information, contact Evangelical Alliance at 186 Kennington Park Road, London, SE11 4BT or visit their website: www.eauk.org

[2] All addresses of websites listed in this book were accessed at the end of January 2006. However, please bear in mind that some of these sites may move their material to new locations in the future.

Acknowledgements

I am extremely grateful to all the writers who have contributed to this book, and to the series as a whole. It is a joy to work with people who are so committed to thoroughly analysing facets of our culture in order to help Christians in their discipleship and evangelism, and to help those who are not yet Christians begin to see the extraordinary relevance of the Christian faith.

Particular thanks go to Nick Pollard whose insightful writing is the foundation for the books, and who provides many helpful suggestions on material for inclusion. Thanks also to Steve Couch, Managing Editor of Damaris Books, for his constant support during the many stages of pulling the books together, and to the team at Authentic Media who handle the production of the books and with whom we enjoy a strong partnership.

Introduction

'I was scared, really scared, it seemed evil. My friends told me that it was just a trick, but I'm not so sure – I think there might be something in it.' In that one sentence the girl sitting next to me on the train to London had not only opened up her heart and her need for some help and reassurance, she had also opened up two important avenues for conversation. And so we spent most of the rest of the journey talking together about those two issues: the nature of evil and the nature of spiritual reality.

The conversation began because she was talking about the 'live' séance carried out by Derren Brown on Channel Four in May 2004. This programme, called *Séance*, was, at that time, the third most complained about show in British television history – and was also one of the most talked about. But the two issues she raised are relevant to most films and programmes about the supernatural, and they are well worth helping people to explore.

First, what is evil? The girl on the train was scared by the séance because she felt that there was something evil in it. There is no doubt that when the media explore the supernatural they usually dwell on the subject of evil. This focus may make for exciting drama, but it also reinforces an increasingly popular view of evil that sees it as something inevitable and inescapable. This is often expressed in a phrase such as 'you can't have good without evil'.

Philosophically, this view of evil is rooted in a form of dualism which views good and evil as necessary, equal and opposite forces. This idea has become so engrained in our culture that it influences many film-makers and book authors. Consequently, their films and books further reinforce the idea in popular culture. For example, it tends to lead them towards writing a climax of the story which seeks to resolve the tension between the so-called equal forces of good and evil by establishing a balance between them, rather than through the triumph of good over evil. Therefore, people are left with the idea that evil will always be there, lurking over your shoulder, and there is nothing you can do to overcome it. That is not what the Bible tells us.

Then comes the next question: what is spiritual reality anyway? Derren Brown would deny that he was doing anything evil because he claims that he does not do anything supernatural. After the séance, he said that he was simply showing how people can be tricked into false beliefs. Apparently, Derren used to be a Christian, but he doesn't seem to believe in any spiritual reality now. He declares that, 'Blind faith is something we need to grow out of.' There certainly is truth in that statement. Blind faith is not helpful. But that does not mean that all faith is blind.

Clearly, there is blindness on both sides of the argument about spiritual reality. Many people believe or disbelieve because of preconceptions and assumptions.

That is why we need to help one another to think about *why* we believe or disbelieve, to have open minds, and to at least explore the possibility of a genuine supernatural, spiritual reality.

The girl on the train was at least open to considering the possibility of a spiritual reality. What she didn't know was where she should look in order to find it. As we talked, she began to see the possibility that it might be worth looking for answers in the life and teaching of Jesus. Indeed, she even began to see that, if the things Jesus said and did were true, then it might be possible that evil could be overcome rather than just balanced.

When we began the conversation, she was in the same position as many people whom I meet day by day. Often the films and television programmes they have watched, or the books they have read, have begun to open an interest in spiritual things – but they are confused and concerned. That is why we need to help them to think through the issues. And we will be better able to help them if we have done some of that thinking ourselves. That is what this book is designed to help you to do.

Nick Pollard

I'm a rational person. I believe in science. I don't believe in the paranormal and I don't believe in ghosts.

Dr Miranda Grey in the film *Gothika*

1. Deliver Us From Evil

Nick Pollard

It was Christmas Eve. This is the day on which, traditionally, husbands realise they still have not bought a present for their wives and make a mad dash for the shops. As I drove into the city-centre car park, I noticed two vehicles bumper to bumper across a parking space. They had both tried to grab that spot but, coming from different directions, they had met in the middle – and neither would give an inch. Within moments, their confrontation increased from honking horns, to revving engines, to shouting and swearing – even to threats of violence. Meanwhile, neither of the drivers had noticed that, all around them, parking spaces were becoming available (including the one that I parked in easily). They were missing them all.

As I walked away from my car to the shops, I reflected on how those men's behaviour had been such a clear picture of human nature. There in the car park was a demonstration, not just of the tendency for the evil of hostility and violence that each of us has, but also the way in which we can be so focused on one aspect of our environment that we miss so much of what is available all around us. The drivers saw each other, and they saw red, but they failed to see the available spaces around them. In the same way, many people see the physical world and they become so absorbed in it that they fail to recognise the spiritual, supernatural reality that is all around them.

In this book, we will help you to talk with people about the supernatural, we will see how entirely reasonable it is to talk about the supernatural as a reality, and we will see how this can relate easily to people's felt needs and desires. At the same time, we will also help you to talk about the relationship between the supernatural and evil. In particular, we will help you to talk with people about the nature of evil: what it is and whether it can be overcome.

Much of the way in which we will help you to talk about these issues will be through enabling you to think about how they are explored in contemporary films, books and television programmes. So let's start by looking at two film trilogies that both explore the nature of evil, but present very different perspectives: the *Matrix* trilogy and *The Lord of the Rings*.

Rather like the two men in their cars, many people will have watched these (and other) recent films in a way that misses much of the significance of the storylines. But with a little help from you, they will be able to think more deeply about them. As with all stories, whether expressed in films or books, if we think about them, we can tell quite a lot about the worldview of the author and the culture within which – and for which – he or she is writing. And this can help us to talk about and think about our own worldview, and that of our friends.

Balancing Act

There are a number of similarities between *The Matrix* and *The Lord of the Rings*. They were both trilogies, and were both hugely successful at the box office. They were both broadly in the genre of fantasy adventure, telling the story of a quest towards a goal.[1] In both there are negative, destructive forces and personalities, which represent evil. And in both there are positive, creative forces and personalities, which represent good. Both trilogies build the narrative tension in a struggle between the good and the evil. And then, in both, this tension is finally released at the end when the goal is achieved and the story is resolved.

But what is significant is the difference in the way in which the story is resolved. Evil is dealt with in both trilogies, but in very different ways. In *The Lord of the Rings,* the resolution is achieved through good conquering evil, overcoming it, even destroying it. In the *Matrix* trilogy, on the other hand, there is a very different resolution: evil is not conquered or destroyed; rather it is balanced out by good.[2] These two different storylines demonstrate two very different views of evil and, indeed, two different underlying views about supernatural reality.

In the *Matrix* films, good and evil are presented as equal and opposite forces that co-exist in tension with one another. It is as if they are designed to be together and the world will only properly function if there is a balance between them. The problem arises when the equilibrium is disturbed. This is described very neatly by the character called the Oracle when she says that Neo (the representation of good) and Agent Smith (the representation of evil) are the result of 'equations trying to balance themselves out'. Indeed, in the wider context, this is achieved in the climax of the film when Neo and the all of the artificial intelligence machines agree to abandon their hostilities and live in harmony. So, evil is not destroyed; it is simply brought into a balanced equilibrium with good.

This is a popular idea that has roots in many different philosophies and theologies. Take Neoplatonism, for example.[3] This is a complex (and, in some ways, ambiguous) philosophy, based upon a belief that there are different levels of being which co-exist together. Or look at Zoroastrianism,[4] which is a religious belief with two opposing good and evil deities – Ahura Mazda, meaning 'wise Lord', and Anghra Mainyu, meaning 'destructive spirit'.

Indeed, there are subtle indications of a particular link to one such ancient worldview in the film. The Oracle wears earrings with the yin/yang symbol[5] on them. This well-known Chinese symbol represents the two supposed cosmic forces of creative energy from which everything originates. 'Yin' represents dark, femininity and receptivity; 'yang' represents light, masculinity and activity. The symbol that combines the two together represents the notion that everything originates from, and depends upon, the interaction of these opposite and complementary principles. It is an important aspect of the *Matrix* trilogy, especially in *The Matrix Revolutions.* In the original Chinese philosophy of Taoism, yang and yin do not represent good and evil as we understand it. To call yang 'good' and yin 'evil' would be to misrepresent this ancient worldview. However, whatever the reality, the fact is that many people today think that yin and yang are good and evil. So, when they then equate the (correct) yin/yang concept of interaction and mutual dependence with this (incorrect) representation of good and evil, they absorb the idea that good and evil are equal and opposite forces that co-exist in tension with one another.

This view of evil is one which is increasingly popular in our culture. It is often expressed in conversations by people who say, 'You can't have good without evil.' What they mean by this is that good and evil must exist together in some form of balance. This concept pops up in various forms in many popular films and television programmes. *Star Wars*, for example, contains the prophecy of the one who will 'restore balance to the force'. Meanwhile, *Buffy the Vampire Slayer* contains the character Whistler, whose duty is to maintain the balance between good and evil.

Conflicting Views

On the other hand, the storyline of *The Lord of the Rings* presents a very different view of the conflict between good and evil. Here, evil is recognised as a corruption of good. In the story, we see how good people's hearts can be turned to evil. Such is the power of the ring that has corrupted Gollum, and threatens to do the same to Frodo. Gollum is the devious, scheming, pathetic character who is trying to get his hands on the 'precious' ring. But Gollum wasn't always like that. He was once a young hobbit-like creature called Smeagol who enjoyed his life with his cousin Deagol. One day, while fishing, Deagol saw something shiny in the water, pulled it out and found it was a beautiful gold ring. Without even knowing what this ring could do, Smeagol was overcome with a desire to own it himself, and he murdered his cousin so he could take it. Thus began the descent of Smeagol, as his good nature was corrupted into evil.

Similarly, once Frodo has the ring, he, too, is often tempted to use its magical powers and we see the potential of its power to corrupt him. But Frodo resists and, when someone is required to take the ring to the place where it can be destroyed, it is Frodo who steps forward. Thus begins his long journey, which we watch throughout the trilogy. It is clear that the goal of the story is not to somehow find a balance between good and evil, but rather to overcome evil and destroy it. Thus, in the film, they are not looking for a way in which good and evil uses of the ring can co-exist together. They know that this is not possible. The ring – and the evil that it represents – must be completely destroyed. This view of evil is much more consistent with the biblical Christian understanding of good and evil. This is not surprising since Tolkein was a Christian and was writing in, and for, a largely Christian culture.

In Christian theology, evil is recognised as a perversion of goodness. Evil is parasitic upon good. Accordingly, evil is not a fundamental reality; it has not always existed. It came about through the corruption of good, when angels and then humans turned away from God. Therefore, according to this understanding of evil, it cannot exist on its own. And it does not need to exist at all. Despite what people popularly express, according to Christian theology, you *can* have good without evil.

Good News About Good

This is a great message for us all to know. It is a wonderful story for us to tell people. But when we do so, we need to be clear about what we mean. In Christian theology, the victory of good over evil is brought about by God. It is made possible because of

Jesus' death on the cross, not by what we have done or can do. We will see elements of this victory becoming apparent in our own lives as God works in our hearts through his Holy Spirit, and we will see elements of it in this world as we pray for it and obey God's call to 'do what is right, to love mercy, and to walk humbly with [our] God' (Mic. 6:8). But it is not up to us to seek to destroy evil in our own strength. Part of this story was brought to many people's attention in the recent popular film adaptation of C.S. Lewis's classic story *The Lion, the Witch and the Wardrobe*. Here, Aslan the lion provides a representation of Jesus when he willingly gives himself to be killed by the White Witch. However, the victory that this death brings is then worked out in a physical battle in which the children take sword and bow to destroy the forces of evil.

Perhaps there are parallels here with President George Bush's use of the term 'axis of evil' when he referred to Iraq and its allies. Having identified this 'evil', he then invaded with guns and bombs in his attempt to destroy it. And perhaps there are parallels with the cases of children harmed, or even killed, by people claiming that the child was possessed by evil and needed to have it driven out. There have recently been high-profile stories of cases where an apparent attempt at exorcism led to injury or death of the child. The exorcists said they were seeking to destroy evil – but in fact they were destroying the life of the child. The tragic nature of such events was brought to many more people's attention through the recent film *The Exorcism of Emily Rose* (based on a true story).[6] In this story, a priest is accused of negligence resulting in the death of a young college student who thought that she was possessed and turned to him to have the demons exorcised.

Faith in the Dock

With such films and such true news stories circulating in our culture, perhaps it is not surprising that many then take the view that this kind of religious belief in the supernatural is itself evil. Indeed, they propose that any belief in the supernatural is damaging to us because it stops us from seeing the world as it really is – a natural material world. One such person is the Charles Simonyi Professor of the Public Understanding of Science at Oxford University, Richard Dawkins. Dawkins is an enthusiastic advocate of Darwin's theory of evolution by natural selection and has written about this at length. But he doesn't just stop there – he moves on to argue that an alternative belief in divine creation is not only untrue, but also deeply damaging to people and to our world.

He has expressed this view in many lectures and books, but he particularly brought it into popular culture in his two-part look at religion, called *The Root of all Evil?*[7] In these programmes, he challenged what he describes as a process of non-thinking called faith. He is astonished that people today still believe in religion, despite the knowledge about rational, scientific truth. In the first programme, he took the viewer on a tour of believers from the three Abrahamic faiths: Judaism, Islam and Christianity. He sought to show that, although religions may preach morality, peace and hope, in fact they bring intolerance, violence and destruction. Therefore, he said, 'the war between good and evil is really just the war between two evils.'

As always, the ideas which Richard Dawkins propounds have a great effect upon people. But they suffer from the same set of logical fallacies which he falls into time after time.[8] For example, his accusation that religious belief in the supernatural is evil suffers from the logical fallacy known as 'self-contradiction'. This fallacy points out that a statement cannot be true if it contradicts itself. For example, imagine I tell you that, 'I cannot speak a word of English.' That statement cannot possibly be true, since I am speaking English in order to make the statement. Thus the statement contradicts itself and cannot be true.

When Dawkins argues that we evolved through survival of the fittest *and* that religious belief is evil, he, too, is contradicting himself. By claiming that religious belief is evil, he is assuming that evil is a real, meaningful concept. Thus, he is arguing that a moral right and a moral wrong actually exist. But can he do that if he believes that we have evolved, through unguided, undirected, natural selection of random mutations? There are many philosophers who say that he can't. They point out that the concepts of right, wrong, good and evil only make sense if God exists. This is sometimes expressed in what is called the 'Moral Argument for God' which might be expressed as follows:

- Activities such as torturing babies for fun are objectively morally wrong and we really ought not to do them
- Therefore, because of this and other examples, we can know that there are certain things that are objectively morally wrong and we really ought not to do them.

Before moving on, we need to unpack the three concepts in that sentence: the concepts of *morally wrong, objectively* and *ought*:

- If there is something that is *morally wrong* then there must be a moral law-giver. This is because something cannot be right or wrong without someone or something (whether outside or inside of us) declaring that thing to be right or wrong.

- If the right or wrong is *objective*, then the moral law-giver must be outside of ourselves and must be infinite. This is because the fact that it is objective means that it goes beyond individual human preference or personality or culture. Therefore, it cannot be finite like us human beings – it must be infinite.

- Finally, if we *ought* to obey that law then the infinite law-giver must be personal. This is because if we *ought* to do something, it means that we must be *obligated* to do it – and we cannot be obligated to something impersonal, only something personal.

So, the argument continues:

- The fact that there are certain things that are objectively morally wrong, and we ought not to do them, means that there must be a personal, infinite moral law-giver
- That is, there must be a God.

Now, whatever we think of the conclusiveness of that moral argument for God, we can see what will happen if we turn it round the other way. Let's work from Dawkins's supposed non-existence of God to see whether he *can* then believe in the existence of a real right and wrong, let alone the concept of something being evil.

Ignoring the Evidence

According to Dawkins, we evolved by survival of the fittest. Therefore, there can be no one to obligate us such that we really ought to do or not do something.

Of course, we might have evolved in such a way that we happen to not do something, or we might live in a society in which other people have evolved such that they try to force us not to do something. But we cannot really be *obligated* not to do it. In an atheistic evolutionary world, things just are the way they are. If there was no purpose in our evolution, there can be no concept of the way things 'ought to be'.

What is more, if our evolution took place solely through the entirely natural selection of random mutations, then there can be no objective source of right and wrong.[9] We can talk about how things are for some people, and compare that with how they are for other people. We can even talk about how things make us better fitted for survival. But we can never talk about whether things are *objectively* morally right or wrong. If there was no design behind our evolution, then there can be no objective template against which to judge anything as absolutely right or wrong. Therefore, if Dawkins is right to believe that there is no God, then there can be no real law-giver, because there is no real right and wrong, and no one to whom we are really obligated. So, how can Dawkins talk about anything being evil? Surely, even any use of that term contradicts his belief about reality.

His self-contradiction doesn't stop there, however. In the programmes, he repeated his regular criticism of religious faith as being 'belief without, even in spite of, evidence'. This seems to be his own made-up definition of faith – and certainly not one that any theologian would use! He also called people only to believe something if there was scientific evidence for it. By scientific evidence he means some form of experiment that enables us to test the belief in some empirical way. Boiled down to its basic form, Dawkins is saying, 'Only believe something if there is scientific evidence that it is true.'

Unfortunately, yet again Dawkins falls into the fallacy of self-contradiction. When telling us, 'only believe something if there is scientific evidence that it is true,' he is telling us to *believe something* (that we should only believe something if there is scientific evidence that it is true). Now, we might reasonably ask him to tell us what scientific evidence he can give us for this belief. Can he provide some scientific evidence for the truth of the statement that we should 'only believe something if there is scientific evidence that it is true'? Of course, he is unable to give us any. That statement is not verifiable scientifically. It is an expression of his belief – a statement of his faith.

This Means Nothing to Me

Dawkins is not alone in this self-contradiction. In the last century, there was a group of people who fell into this trap. They called themselves the Vienna Circle. They were a number of academics who met in Vienna University in the 1920s and 1930s, mainly under the instigation of Moritz Schlick. They gave birth to the philosophy known as *logical positivism* with its central belief in the *verification principle*. This principle argued that no statement is meaningful if it cannot be verified empirically.[10]

Of course, since then, many philosophers have recognised that their statement of the verification principle was self-contradictory, since the principle itself could not be verified empirically. But that did not stop them from using it to launch attacks on religious beliefs in general – and on belief in the supernatural in particular. They argued that, thanks to the verification principle, a belief in the supernatural is meaningless. They didn't worry about whether it was true or false; as far as they were concerned, it simply did not make sense.

And although many philosophers today would not accept this logical positivist rejection of belief in the supernatural, the fact that Dawkins receives so much air time for essentially the same argument means that it is still a live issue in our contemporary popular culture.

That is bad news in the sense that it means many people are absorbing Dawkins's view that the supernatural does not exist and that religious belief is evil. But it is also good news in that it means that people are ready and willing to talk about the supernatural in general, and evil in particular. And we have a lot we can talk with them about in this area – much of which is covered in the pages of this book.

Notes

1 More than simply being fantasy adventure, they both fit very well with the fundamental structure of a hero myth as outlined by Joseph Campbell in his *Hero with a Thousand Faces* (first published in 1949). He said that all such tales are expressions of what he called the 'Monomyth'. In fact, *The Matrix* seems to have been very deliberately drawing on Campbell's ideas. For more on this, see Steve Couch (ed.), *Matrix Revelations: A thinking fan's guide to the Matrix trilogy* (Damaris, 2003), p. 39–41, 192

2 See Tony Watkins, 'Red Pill, Blue Pill: Conclusion' in Steve Couch (ed.), *Matrix Revelations,* p. 199–207

3 Neoplatonism was shaped by Plotinus (c. AD 205–270) and then modified by many others. Plotinus took the philosophy of Plato (c. 428–348 BC) and combined it together with

Pythagorean, Aristotelian and Stoic thought. For more information, see www.wikipedia.org/wiki/Neoplatonism

[4] An ancient Persian religion based on the teachings of Zoroaster (although this is the Greek version of his name – he was actually known as Zarathushtra). For more information, see www.avesta.org and www.wikipedia.org/wiki/Zoroastrianism

[5] It is properly called the *Taijitu*.

[6] For more on this film, see chapter six.

[7] *The Root of All Evil?*, Channel 4, 9, 16 January 2006

[8] For an article identifying a range of Dawkins's logical fallacies see Peter S. Williams, 'Darwin's Rottweiler and the Public Understanding of Scientism', *Access Research Network* – www.arn.org/docs/williams/pw_dawkinsfallacies.htm

[9] This is not to say that a process of evolution is incompatible with the existence of God, but that Dawkins only sees it in atheistic terms. Whether or not God *did* create through a process of evolution (neither blind nor unguided, because not entirely 'natural') is another question entirely.

[10] To understand more about logical positivism and the problems with the verification principle, see chapter nine.

I couldn't let go of my faith. But what is more interesting is that I don't think God will let go of me.

Bono

2. More Than Meets the Eye – A Biblical Perspective on the Supernatural

Ian Hamlin

Scene One

Last week I was in a gathering of local church leaders – a regular monthly get-together to share stories, arrange meetings, catch up on news, etc. Most of us were present, representing the three Anglican, two Baptist, Roman Catholic, Methodist and United Reformed Churches of our area. All very convivial over tea and biscuits. When our business was over, the host offered a brief 'Thought for the Day' type of epilogue, as is our custom. His theme: the degree to which our churches are considered 'approachable', prompted by a chance conversation with a hair-dresser who had remarked as to how she had 'almost phoned the vicar' over a personal crisis in her life, but had then thought better of it. His challenge: how many of us had received unsolicited calls from those unconnected to our churches, calling on us in their hour of need? The response: minimal – until we began to think a little more, and started to recall stories, people, incidents over the years in our different ministries and very different churches. And then a theme began to emerge. It seemed that the vast majority of these contacts, for each of us, were concerned with one issue: unexplained spiritual presences in their homes. Strange feelings, cold sensations, moving objects, hauntings, ghosts, poltergeists, whatever. What's all that about then? Our theologies of the matter varied, but it seemed this was the main reason why those outside the Church called us up – the one thing they felt it still worthwhile to bother the vicar with.

Scene Two

The week before this meeting I was away for a few days on the South Devon coast. There is something about the more rugged parts of the British coastline in late autumn and early winter. Gone are any signs of soft, summer gentility; the deck chair hawkers and ice-cream sellers have packed up their wares; no more sun-bathers being lulled to sleep by the softly lapping surf. Now there is a beautiful brutality about the place. The salt sea stings your face as you brace yourself against its spray. The biting wind lashes the waves against the huge rocks placed deliberately in a doomed attempt to protect the towering cliffs from the ever-surging sea. The mist, the noise, the taste of the place, all speak of elemental forces. Human influence is dwarfed by something more basic, more powerful, more permanent – something with a hint of glory. I wonder what the steady stream of well-wrapped walkers make of it all?

Scene Three

I'm in my favourite chair. Over these few weeks – as well as attending work meetings and taking short breaks – I read my newspaper, watch the television and generally carry on as in any other period of my life. And, like any other period, from the comfort of my living room, I am constantly introduced to a world of unimaginable horror – a world where mothers of five are gunned down, teenage models are brutally murdered in suburban backwaters, schoolgirls are stabbed in dinner queues, and buggy-pushing parents are assaulted in country lanes. It is my world. And as I read, facts are relayed, investigations are reported, grief is observed, opinions fly like confetti. But underlying it all is an unspoken question: What sort of a world is this? How can we account for all of this when we know that most people are just like us – far from perfect but seeking to do the best we can, in an environment which could always be better but still has plenty to enjoy about it? Frequently, as commentators scratch their collective heads, they, and we, are forced, sometimes reluctantly, to say it is just plain evil. Something malevolent is out there, attached to, but separate from, any single individual – something we cannot quite put our finger on, but that distorts, corrupts and undermines our best intentions to be the sort of people, the sort of community, the sort of world we want to be and know we're capable of becoming. It's almost as if it's a spiritual thing.

Spiritual Reality

Christian churches would seem to be natural places to explore some of these spiritual impulses, and indeed they are. But at times, they, too, can become victims of their age. In his presentation of the Alpha Course, Nicky Gumbel tells a story of an Anglican church which is clearly sceptical of new trends. In a bold assertion of traditional values it affirms: 'Nothing supernatural goes on here!' Quite what God made of that is unrecorded.

It is now as commonplace and unremarkable to refer to our visible, material world as the be-all and end-all of everything as it would have been novel just a few centuries ago. Certainly in biblical times, no explanation would have been considered necessary for the assumption of a worldview which affirmed the existence of a reality beyond the horizon of our sensory perception. The acknowledgement of the presence of spiritual reality, though variously understood, has been a given of human thinking around the world through the vast majority of our history.

Chief among these considerations, of course, has been the person and place of God. Though not the only character in the story, he clearly is the main player and, indeed, writer, producer and director as well. If we are to understand any truth about spiritual reality, he must be our reference point. When it comes to the nature of God, the Bible is unequivocal: God is spirit (Jn. 4:24; Acts 17:24). Yet he has a name, a character, a personality. Clearly this spiritual nature is not vague and nebulous, but of a particular nature. If we understand that, it may open the door to appreciating, discerning and experiencing the fullness of our lives as human beings made in his image.

God Over All

First of all, God is separate from the world he has made (Is. 55:8–9; Ps. 113:4–6; Jn. 8:23). This transcendence locates God outside of our immediate vicinity and marks him out as different from us – not only quantitatively (by degree), but qualitatively too (in very essence).

Specifically, he is referred to as 'above' us. This is hardly surprising, not only given the assumptions about the physical world when the Bible was written, but also because of the theological points that were being made. God's holiness, authority, majesty and all his other attributes make it entirely appropriate for him to be referred to as 'elevated', quite apart from any cosmological naivety. It is because of this essentially spiritual nature of God that this quality of transcendence can only refer to his distinctiveness, not his location. If God is not physical, he cannot be spatial and so be tracked down by any set of coordinates.

God's spiritual otherness, though, does not mean that he is at all distant, remote or unknowable. The balancing item to his transcendence is his immanence. The Bible is just as insistent that the foundational, spiritual reality that is God is always right here, right now (Ps. 139:7–10; Acts 17:27–28). This strand of biblical teaching affirms God's presence and activity in the material world, both in so-called 'secular' human activity and in nature (Rom. 1:19–20). Taken to an extreme, it would equate to a form of pantheism, where God and the world become one and the same. This type of thinking, though popular in a materialistic world increasingly concerned with its environment and other issues that seem 'extra-material' (in the sense of being outside of the scope of the things which this worldview has hitherto considered significant), ultimately reduces God to that of humanity's highest aspiration and achievement. A biblical balance of immanence and transcendence shares the pantheist conviction that nature minus God equals nothing, but in pantheism the reverse is also true, whereas the biblical vision affirms the spiritual reality of God as remaining even after all of creation is gone.

This balance, then, is crucial to maintain (Jer. 23: 23–24), both for our understanding of God, and for an appreciation of the proper place of the spiritual in our experience. That place is not a specific location at all: not heaven rather than earth or vice versa, not the meadow rather than the city, the church over the market square, the individual psyche over the human community. It is always and everywhere. Yet even in the sum total of all of these places, the reality of God is not exhausted for he lives beyond them, authoritative and independent. No wonder our experience of him is so universal and all-encompassing, yet still awesome and mysterious.

The Bible, therefore, reveals God as the spiritual agent, identified both as immanent and transcendent. The distinct spiritual realm, reflected in his transcendence, is every bit as real as the material world of his immanence. This understanding is shown clearly in the most complete demonstration of both the nature of God and the potential of human beings – the life of Jesus.

Danger Zone

Notwithstanding this background, the Christian Church has, at times, responded to the expression and manifestation of spiritual reality with suspicion, revulsion and hostility. From medieval witch hunts to reactions to Harry Potter, fear has often dominated. Of course, this is not the whole story. Throughout Christian history there have been sectors of the Church which have both resisted the extremes of paranoia and also actively sought the positive power of God in every sense. The renewal of interest in the theology of the Holy Spirit and the enormous growth of Pentecostalism in the last century supply ample evidence for this. There are, however, good reasons why Christians have sought to be both careful and discerning in these areas.

The Bible, whilst avoiding a crude dualism that affirms the spiritual over the material, or vice versa, always recognises an essential ambiguity about spiritual power. There is light and dark, good and evil in the spiritual realm (Zech. 3:1; Mt. 4:1; Acts 26:18). Indeed, this distinction is in direct parallel with – even in some sense the source of – the struggle between these forces in all of our everyday lives. This relationship is no doubt the reason why these themes consistently feature in the art, music and film of our culture. They supply a fascinating, dramatic and imaginative setting for fundamental truths of our own experience to be played out.

The dangers inherent in an undiscerning engagement with spiritual forces are clearly laid out in the Bible. It is these scriptural prohibitions that have formed the basis of much of the historic scepticism that I have remarked upon. The clearest overall statement comes in Deuteronomy 18:9–12. Here, although the specific details of the individual practices which are forbidden have been lost, the general point is clear. God's people are to be distinctive, different from the previous occupants of the land, the Canaanites. Their old ways of relating to the spiritual world appeared to be based upon a desire for direct consultation with this separate realm with a view, principally, to discovering and influencing future events. Because of the unique and particular relationship of God's people with God himself, who holds the future in his hands, this former expression of spirituality is considered to be a retrograde step akin to idolatry – the selfish superstitions of a faithless people.

These warnings and prohibitions are repeated often throughout the Old Testament. They are part of the basis upon which the faithfulness of leaders is judged.

Among others, Ahab and Jezebel in Israel (2 Kgs. 9:22), and Manasseh of Judah (2 Kgs. 21:6) are condemned on this basis. It is also given as one of the reasons why the whole nation of Israel is taken into exile (2 Kgs. 17:17–20).

Similarly, in the New Testament the difference between appropriate and inappropriate engagement with the spiritual world is drawn out. In two particular stories in the book of Acts the distinction is made clear. Both Simon (Acts 8:9–25) and Elymas (Acts 13: 6–12) were sorcerers whose methods and motivations were contrasted and compared to Peter's and Paul's respectively. They were found wanting, chiefly because their desire to seek the spiritual was prompted by self-aggrandisement, not a seeking after truth.

In our own very different times, it remains true that many spiritual practices, whether expressed through spiritualism, horoscopes or whatever, have at their root, not a desire to relate to a living God, but an impatient and selfish concern to turn the future our way. As such, they stand in opposition to the biblical model.

Dancing with the Devil[1]

We have already mentioned how the world of the supernatural provides rich pickings for contemporary writers and film-makers to explore ancient stories of good and evil, even to the extent of suggesting the ultimate source of these qualities. We have also recognised how both the undeniable existence of evil and the desire to deflect its impact in the future have caused both reflection on spiritual reality and active involvement with it. These instinctive associations have a biblical basis and so it would seem wise to consider what the Bible has to say about the origin, nature and future destiny of evil.

From the very beginning, the Bible understands evil as more than just unfortunate moral lapses, or even the sum total of the bad things people do. In the story of Adam and Eve, the serpent appears, as an outside agent, to influence, disrupt and destroy the goodness of original creation (Gen. 3). This account is generally called 'the Fall' as it is intended to be descriptive of something fundamental about human experience, then and now. This image of evil as a devious player in the spiritual battleground, which undergirds everyday material existence, is basic to the Bible's understanding (Job 1:7; Lk. 4:13; 1 Jn. 3:8) and has resonated richly with people's experience ever since.

The character of the serpent, however, was only the start. Various artistic impressions of the Devil over the centuries mean that almost everyone has a clear mental image of what he's supposed to look like, but the Bible does not bother with such conjecture. Its concern is not so much with his appearance as his activity. As such the Devil is described as a liar and a murderer (Jn. 8:44), a betrayer (Lk. 22:3), a destroyer (1 Pet. 5:8), an accuser (Rev. 12:10) an imprisoner (Lk. 13:16), a tempter (1 Cor. 7:5), and an overarching enemy (Mt. 13:39). These verses give a fairly full picture of the Devil's agenda. They form a sad but familiar litany of human experience, and affirm that the ultimate origin of these things lies in a suprahuman power.

In the New Testament, although the specific serpent image is repeated (Rev. 20:2), additional emphasis is placed upon the corporate and collective expression of Satanic influence. Paul talks of sin and the law in these terms (Rom. 6:12–23; 7:5–11). He also recognises that the constant human struggle for that which is good and right is a fundamentally spiritual battle (Eph. 6:12). The 'powers' referred to in Ephesians 6 have been the subject of much debate in recent years.[2] Occasionally, it is suggested that they relate to the structures of human society – the religious, intellectual, political and moral forces operating within any culture. Such references as there are to these forces, however, would suggest a more ambiguous understanding, encompassing both human structures and a distinct transcendent dimension (1 Cor. 2:8; Tit. 3:1; Rom. 8:38).

This talk of forces and powers, though, ought not to detract from the accompanying biblical affirmation of evil as demonic, and as the Devil as a person. Though reluctant to afford Satan the dignity that personality suggests, this insight affirms the nature of our experience of evil as prideful, arrogant and rebellious, as well as concurring with the scriptural testimony (1 Jn. 3:8; Lk. 10:18).

The Root of Evil

These insights into the supernatural and spiritual nature of evil also give some clues as to its origin. The fundamental source of evil in the universe is, of course, a difficult and complex matter, culturally and theologically. There are, however, only a few logical possibilities.

First, we might say that it is just one of those mysteries which is impossible for us to get to the bottom of. This is a humble and honest viewpoint, and it is certainly the case that there will always be much that we do not understand. However, given the biblical material we have to work with and the importance of the issue, it seems inadequate.

Second, *metaphysical dualism* suggests that the battle between good and evil is an eternal one in that there exist two opposing and closely matched forces in the very fabric of the universe. This is a popular view, the underlying premise of much thought and many stories. Yet it denies the basic supremacy of God and is not an accurate reflection of the Bible's witness.

Third, *monism* goes to the other extreme and, in affirming the total authority of God, makes evil directly attributable to his will. This presents obvious difficulties with God's consistent opposition to evil and so must also be treated with much suspicion. In a similar way, the popular contemporary idea that evil's origin has to do with the necessary structure of created reality – that somehow God had to do it this way, despite everything – also does not absolve God of ultimate responsibility, even though it is a little more subtle.

Fourth, the traditional view is that evil stems from the misuse of creaturely freedom. Human sinfulness has long been considered in this way, stemming from the Fall of Genesis 3. A similar scenario can be painted which sources transcendent sin in a parallel situation. In other words, human failure – Adam's and ours – does not provide the ultimate origin of evil, but pinpoints our becoming implicated in an existing rebellion in the spiritual realm. There are passages in the Bible which point towards just such a circumstance (Is. 14:12; Jude 6; 2 Pet. 2:4), but they are by no means watertight and are insufficient in themselves to provide a fully-fledged doctrine of an angelic fall. However, given the logical and theological possibilities we have briefly discussed, they offer an intriguing insight.

In our discussion of the origin and nature of evil we have perhaps run the risk of giving the Devil too much credit. The dominant focus of the New Testament when it comes to the subject of supernatural evil is its absolute and definite defeat. In Revelation a picture is painted of a renewed creation completely free from the negative influences we have been talking of (Rev. 21: 2–4). The key moment in this victory was the cross of Jesus. Whatever else it did, the death and resurrection of Jesus claimed and secured an eternal triumph over all the forces of evil (Col. 2:14–15). This was not an additional afterthought in the ministry of Jesus, though. The gospels are clear that it was a fundamental part of his mission from the beginning. In Luke's gospel, we see his overcoming of the temptation in the wilderness at the outset of his work (Lk. 4:1–13) and the consistent engagement directly with demonic powers in a number of miraculous encounters (Lk. 4:31–37; 8:26–39; 9:37–43; 11:14–28). In John's gospel, Jesus is unequivocal, he was about winning an eternal victory (Jn. 12:30–31). Despite the certainty and the completeness of the triumph won at the cross, the Bible is under no illusions as to the ongoing struggle that is experienced (2 Cor. 4:4). Theologian Oscar Cullmann famously likened this to the period between D-day and VE day during the Second World War.[3] At the first, victory was indisputably secured, but battles still raged and casualties continued to suffer until the curtain was finally drawn on the enemy's vicious, but futile, struggle.

Spirits in the Material World

We have now considered the underlying spiritual reality in which the Bible sets itself. We have looked at the warnings it gives as to indiscriminate engagement with spiritual power. We have also reflected on the way in which it sets its basic story of the goodness of God securing a lasting victory over all that threatens it, in a profoundly spiritual setting – despite that triumph being won amidst the very earthy dust of a Jerusalem hillside. To conclude, we shall briefly examine the examples of two biblical heroes who were called to live very practically in an environment full of supernatural threats and spiritual danger.

Joseph and Daniel are indisputably two of the most familiar and celebrated of biblical characters. With their multi-coloured coat and lion-filled den they have become Sunday school standard-bearers, often held up as the very epitome of God-fearing faithfulness. They both lived, however, in alien cultures where they were politically marginalised and spiritually threatened. The supernatural, spiritual forces which we have been considering were dominant, blatant and antagonistic towards the exclusive and devoted worship of the one true God whom they served.

Joseph, sold into slavery in the most powerful nation on earth, threw himself into his unfamiliar surroundings and prospered. Furthermore, this success was readily attributed to spiritual causes (Gen. 39:2–6). His moral certainty, again a consequence of his faith, caused him to be imprisoned, yet, as before, his spiritual giftedness ensured not only his survival, but his elevation. Joseph's ability to interpret dreams was a rich currency in Pharaoh's court and, in direct competition with 'all the magicians and wise men of Egypt' (Gen. 41:8), he was vindicated once again. The long and tortuous story of Joseph ends with the extraordinary scene of his father Jacob granting a blessing upon Pharaoh himself (Gen. 47:10).

Similarly, Daniel was hauled from his comfort zone and asked to live out his faith in the pagan surroundings of Babylon.[4] As with Joseph, Daniel enthusiastically embraced his situation and immersed himself in this very different culture and way of life. He learnt the language and studied the literature, yet he drew the line at eating the royal food (Dan. 1:3–8). At the end of his three-year training Daniel's insight was found to be 'ten times better than that of all the magicians and enchanters' (Dan. 1:20). His supernatural perception earned him the respect of court over the assorted magicians, enchanters astrologers and diviners whose territory he was undoubtedly treading all over, and he eventually became their chief (Dan. 5:11). From Daniel's testimony, the King consistently, though hardly faithfully, acknowledged his God as supreme.

Both these stories are spiritually complicated, drenched in irony, and full of potential misinterpretations. Faced with such situations, the easiest option is to compromise, blend in and assimilate. No doubt there were those who pointed the finger at Joseph and Daniel in this regard. Encountering spiritual reality, like many other things, can be moulded to become non-threatening, comfortable and easily explained. Much of religious history has been the story of that process and, in our own times, the popularity of a 'pick-and-mix' type of spirituality with all the awkward or challenging bits removed, continues in the same way.

On the other hand, it is also a very real option to become negative and critical, retreating into an exclusive spiritual ghetto in an attempt to keep pure. The consequent ineffectiveness, or even persecution, being considered a spiritual badge of martyrdom. Had Joseph or Daniel had the benefit of our Bibles in their hands, they could easily have found several texts to seemingly support such a standpoint, yet they consistently resisted it. They knew that their specific calling was to draw upon the resources which God had given them to further his agenda in the place where they found themselves.

As we conclude this reflection on the biblical material available to us, we must ask the question: What would it have us do? How, in the light of all that we have learnt, should we approach the spiritual climate in which we live at the beginning of the twenty-first century? The answers seem clear. Never underestimate the power of spiritual reality – its fact, its impact and its relevance remains profoundly significant. Exercise caution when engaging with such powers – the biblical warnings and prohibitions are there for good reason, and we are called to be wise and discerning in all of these matters. This is certainly not an appropriate arena for showmanship, bravado or self-aggrandisement. We should also recognise the dimensions of the battle we are in, that the struggles we, and those around us, face are multi-faceted and, often, deep rooted. Ultimately, though, our attitude should be one of celebration: a fundamental victory has already been won which we should increasingly see filtering through into every aspect of our lives, and we have access to resources, beyond the material, to equip us to live effective lives.

As we face the challenge of living in a spiritually diverse and complicated culture, we can do so confidently and wisely, not cowering from the threat of the difficulties or bemoaning the absence of perfection. Without naivety or cynicism, we are called to engage positively in the world as it is, knowing that it is not all there is.

Notes

[1] For several of the ideas in this section I am indebted to Nigel Wright and, in particular, his book *The Fair Face of Evil: Putting the Power of Darkness in Its Place* (Marshall Pickering, 1989).

[2] See especially Walter Wink's trilogy, *Naming the Powers* (Augsburg Fortress, 1984), *Unmasking the Powers* (Augsburg Fortress, 1986) and *Engaging the Powers* (Augsburg Fortress, 1990).

[3] Oscar Cullmann, *Christ and Time* (London, 1951), p. 198

[4] For a helpful reflection on Daniel's life as a model for contemporary living see Viv Thomas, *Second Choice*, (Paternoster Press, 2000).

Something that looks like a miracle turns out to be dead simple.

Saint Peter in the film *Millions*

3. Entertaining Doubt

Mark Stafford

The funny thing about our twenty-first century society is that we are caught between the facts we think we know, and the sneaking feelings we can't quite shake off. The old biblical request – 'I do believe; help me overcome my unbelief!'[1] – is almost entirely reversed in our collective psyche: for the most part we are unbelievers, but, Lord help us, we still believe. Or so it would seem if the response to Derren Brown's *Séance* is anything to go by.

Over a period of nearly an hour one night in May 2004, we watched a dozen students be told repeatedly that what they were experiencing was an experimental recreation of the sort of séances famously faked by Kate and Margaret Fox in the late nineteenth century. We watched the self-confessed magician and entertainer explain how he had manipulated their choices in ways not dissimilar to those used by the Victorian showmen (and women) who created spirit cabinets, Ouija boards and the like. And we saw twelve ordinary undergraduates become slowly unnerved, and ultimately completely terrified, by what they were experiencing. What's more, we listened to telephone reports from those, like us, 'joining in at home' that seemed to reveal the same strangely child-like reactions: 'Something just moved behind the curtain'; 'My wardrobe just jerked.' At the end of the programme, the woman whose 'spirit' had apparently been communicating from beyond the grave was revealed to be sitting in the van only just beyond the doors of the building. She was no more dead than any of the other victims of the suicide pact made up to create the spooky atmosphere necessary for the show to unfold. The ghost was unmasked, the Scooby snacks were handed round, and everybody laughed and went home a little wiser. Or did they?

There were many people who were concerned about the airing of a 'live séance', who will not have seen anything to allay their fears, and who will not be in any way reassured to know that the show wasn't live at all but recorded weeks before. There are many others who will have watched the programme and ignored all the disclaimers and denouements, remaining convinced that they have just witnessed a supernatural event. And there will have been some present at the filming who still slept with their lights on for days afterwards, despite the reassurances of the production company that it was all make-believe. What makes me so sure of this? Simply the fact that on 21 October 1888, Margaret Fox Kane, whose original séances gave rise to the Spiritualist movement, confessed that she and her sister had been lying and faking all along. And nobody in the world of spiritualism paid the least bit of notice. The movement continued to grow, unfazed by its own basis in fraud, from that era of enlightenment to this age of post-modern cynicism.

It would seem that experiences of what we believe to be supernatural, function much like the insinuations of a cunning courtroom lawyer: it doesn't matter if there is an objection from the other side, nor if that objection is sustained, the impression created cannot easily be undone. Something within us – perhaps long buried – has been stirred, and, like the restless spirits we've been duped into thinking we saw, it is not about to go quietly back into its box.

Séance Fiction

In truth, it is this spirit that animates not only what Derren Brown does on all his shows, but what every magician has ever done – this belief in magic, in hidden powers, that makes even the simplest parlour trick 'work'. If we didn't have a category marked 'mystery' into which we can tuck things we cannot immediately explain, then we would just, well, work them out. We would stop dismissing the simplest solutions and become drawing room Occams,[2] cutting away all but the obvious, and failing to be entertained or amazed. Or afraid. 'Well,' we would be saying, 'you must have another newspaper that looks just like the one you ripped up.' Or, simpler still: 'You must be lying.' That would be the end of the Magic Circle. But this is not what happens. Indeed, it is quite the opposite of what happens. Historian of magic Edward Claflin asks:

> Is a strongly felt illusion any less 'true' than reality? In our history, as we pass easily through time and space, we are searching for the world of that illusion. It is the illusion of magic, and the magic of illusion that we are primarily interested in – not the privy tricks or the key to the secrets themselves. We seek the bafflements, the contradictions . . . *It is not knowledge we are after, but mystery and disguise.* We want to gaze at the impossible. We are hungry for surprise, astonishments.[3]

Because we want 'mystery and disguise', because we want to be astonished, we don't look too closely.

Now enter a magician apparently telling us that there is no mystery, there are no occulted powers, that hocus-pocus is just mumbo-jumbo. What are we to make of this conjuror's slightly surprising testimony? Well, he's lying. Every effect Derren Brown performs depends on the supernatural – on the fundamental and contradictory claim that is at its heart: first, that there is something beyond the edges of what we know; and second, that this thing can, nonetheless, be known, and appropriated.

The mechanics of an illusion depend, of course, on the fact that the magician knows things which are beyond our knowing; that he has more cards up his sleeve; that there is something – or someone – behind the curtain or sitting in the van outside. But the impact of an illusion requires *faith*. It requires that we believe the magician to have access to knowledge which transcends that of ordinary mortals, whether that is the shaman's knowledge of the spirit realm, or the medium's knowledge of the dead, or Mesmer's ether, or Brown's psychological suggestion. It is the tangible evidence of something in which we have come to believe that delights. It is standing in the thrall of a master who can apparently control at will something we have experienced fleetingly or unpredictably that brings the fascinated crowd to the marketplace, and sees us set the maestro on a pedestal. Or a pile of burning twigs.

Orthodox Heretic

This, of course, is precisely where many Christians would cheerfully see Derren Brown for one or other of his heresies (or for both). On the one hand is the claim that there are no demons or ghosts, Holy or otherwise. On the other is his ability to conjure them up all the same in living rooms around the country. But perhaps it would be wise to hold fire a moment. What of this claim, this supposed heresy? He insists that the power of the Ouija board is a combination of trickery and psychology, and insinuates that only once the spirits have been *drained* from our glasses do we begin to imagine that they can *move* them. He is adamant that the dead keep their own counsel; that it is we who tell tales about them. He preaches vehemently against false prophets who claim to bring hope from the Other Side, condemning them as charlatans. And whilst he stops short of describing John Edward as 'the biggest douche in the universe',[4] he clearly shares *South Park* creators Trey Parker and Matt Stone's opinion that the world would be better off recognising that if you hadn't resolved your relationship with the deceased before they died, you've missed your chance.

Is this heretical? It sounds suspiciously like orthodox Christian doctrine. There is nothing in the Christian tradition which suggests that spirits can interfere with material reality. Unlike most belief systems that include the demonic, Christianity has no tales of demons assaulting people, or smashing crockery, or kidnapping children. Indeed, when challenged by a central hero of the faith to produce the most basic demonstration of such powers on Mount Carmel, the flaming emissaries from the fires of hell provide nothing more than a damp squib. Nor do Christians, in theory at least, subscribe to the belief that the dead can be contacted, or might contact us. With one notable exception.

There are only three other stories in Judeo-Christian Scriptures that could be construed as 'ghost stories'.

Two of them, the Transfiguration and the dead roaming Jerusalem in Matthew's crucifixion account, centre on the exception in question, and the other – the account of the Witch of Endor[5] – reads like every tale of 'conversing with a departed soul' through a medium: dubiously dependent on the medium's word and on the credulity of the client. In fact, it is precisely this – human agency – that marks the Christian standpoint on the spirit world. There may be a battle afoot with spiritual powers and authorities, but it is fought in the minds and hearts of flesh and blood people, and with ordinary human speech and action, not bells or incantations; not smoke or mirrors or proton gun streams. Derren Brown is quick to argue that when we think a spirit might be hurling tambourines out of cabinets, further investigation will reveal a human had a hand in it, and whilst Christians may believe that a spirit can move a person to wave a tambourine, those who claim it can move itself are closer to heresy than our cynical TV magician.

Sympathy for the Magician

Is it perhaps the case that the only heretical thing in all this is that Brown doesn't believe in *any* spirit, the God of Abraham included? So he is an atheist, who exposes false gods as precisely that – false. This doesn't seem to fit him very neatly for the role of antichrist. Indeed, it might help us to consider that antichrist is a term best understood not as the *opposite* of Christ (as in antimatter) but as *alternatives* to Christ (as in antipasti). In other words, antichrist is that which purports to offer the same power or reward as the Messiah – false prophets, fakes, pretenders, purveyors of false hope.

These are the very people Brown is eager to unmask. A century earlier, Houdini dedicated himself to a similar mission of exposing fraudulent mediums and miracle workers. A crucial difference, perhaps, was that his belief in the possibility of escaping from the grave was a sincere one, and his demonstrations were motivated (apart from the similarly convenient opportunity for a magician to cash in on contemporary beliefs) by a frustrated desire to find the real thing. It is hard to believe that Derren Brown doesn't share this almost universal human desire – a desire that, as we have seen, underpins the effectiveness of his performance. But he has seen so much that is not the genuine article, and he knows so much about the ways that 'holy' men and women (including Christians) have deceived would-be believers over millennia, that consequently he is reluctant to put his faith in anything. This is no more convincing a reason to demonise him than the fact that he sports a pointy beard.

Far from vilifying this magical celebrity, perhaps Christians ought to welcome his input into the current debate on spirituality – in terms of what he says and what he does not wish to say, what is so eloquently said by the things he does, and how audiences react to them. For as long as human beings have been gathering around flickering lights in the centre of their living spaces, there has been a strongly-recurring theme in the stories they have told: the tale of a life beyond this life; the rumour of a hero that might enter that shadow realm and return with treasures of healing, wisdom, even immortality. Karen Armstrong, writes in her *A Short History of Myth:*

> An experience of transcendence has always been part of the human experience. We seek out moments of ecstasy . . . and if people no longer find [them] in temples, synagogues,

churches or mosques, they look for it elsewhere . . . What
if this world were not all there is? How would this affect
our lives – psychologically, practically or socially? Would
we become different? More complete? And, if we did find
that we were so transformed, would that not show that
our mythical belief was true in some way, that it was
telling us something important about our humanity, even
though we could not prove this rationally?[6]

Armstrong insists that all our mythology tells of
another plane existing alongside our own that in some
sense is deeper and stronger. It all addresses our fear
of extinction; all involves some sort of sacrifice; all
claims to show us how we should act. We have never
stopped welcoming these heroes into our midst, and
only recently started trying to keep the hero, and
something of his story, without allowing either to shape
our behaviour. The trouble is that all heroes, when they
are encased in the kryptonite of specific time and place,
seem to lose their power; every story seems to require
at least one degree of separation to spring to life. So
Christians find that the 'greatest story ever told', their
unique hero himself, stands as in a hall of mirrors,
surrounded by reflections, refractions and distortions
which are virtually indistinguishable from the real. The
fact that there is a popular hero, credited with genuine
powers of his own, running around claiming that there
are nothing but images in Scaramanga's cave,[7] and
cheerfully shooting at mirror after mirror, should not
concern people of faith one iota. The end of this course
of action can only leave one man standing amid the
shards and empty frames – and it will not be James
Bond or John Maclean or Derren Brown. It is not faith
that seeks to prise Brown's weapons from his fingers,
it is lack of faith. Faith is invulnerable to bullets – lead,
silver or otherwise.

Art of Darkness

Ironically, one of the most understandable complaints, about *Séance* in particular, may well founder on the inverse argument. It seems sensible to be concerned that, as no shortage of teenagers claim to have been genuinely disturbed by experiences with a Ouija board, and as evil itself is no myth, anyone claiming convincingly that the effects attributed to Parker Bros.' most controversial game[8] are mere chicanery presents a danger to young minds by seeming to underestimate real evil. But are people more likely to dabble with the famous planchette because they think it is just a bit of fun? Probably not. In fact, quite the contrary. People do not play with Ouija boards because they *don't* think it's real; they play with them because they think it *might* be. It would be easy to assume that it is *lack* of fear that allows adolescents to explore the occult, but generally it is the *presence* of fear that excites this exploration. And, however you view these complexities of our human fascination with taboo, if the general Christian consensus is that the media falsely depict evil as more powerful than the insipid forces of good, and if both the Old and the New Testament are clear that the most potent weapon in the arsenal of Satan is deceiving people (lies, exaggeration and the potential terror or intrigue that ensues) then anyone pulling sheets off supposed ghosts and revealing wires and pulleys would be a friend of the Christian agenda, wouldn't they? The problem, the disquiet, lies in Derren Brown's second 'heresy' – in the fact that he, like Houdini before him, isn't really an exposer of magic at all, but an exponent of it; in the fact, quite simply, that he is an entertainer. For all that his shows, like many sideshows down the centuries, claim to reveal mysteries, they simply and deliberately replace old mysteries with new. And in so doing they raise the spectre of spectres past, summoning from the depths of our psyche things we thought were childish fantasies, ancient history.

You may, of course, feel that this is reason enough to consider the show ill-advised or irresponsible. And if you do, there is little point in emphasising that, in the words of Robert Houdin, 'a magician is an actor playing the part of a magician', because the very thing the magician depends on for his effect is the thing you are concerned about – this ghost, lurking in the dark corners of our beings that is conjured into life by contact, however spurious, with the Beyond.

Perhaps, though, it might be worth wondering why these phantoms continue to linger. Why are we so quick to believe that a wine glass and a set of cards, clearly no older than the magician, hail from 551 BC? And why should that make them any more evocative anyway? Why should the dark and tales of deaths in the building set us so on edge? Why should a man who describes himself as, 'a balding, goateed show-off in a corduroy suit' incite such a strong reaction in the first place? And, above all, why should that reaction outlast even his own testimony that it was all just a trick?

It is in the answers to these questions that the *real* ghosts are to be found. The ghost of a long-lost past when humanity was in permanent contact with the 'supernatural'; the ghost of Eden; the ghost of our childhood acceptance of the obvious truth – that there is more to life than we can know; the ghost of the things we claim not to believe any more. The ghost, in short, of all that is fundamental to the human person, which cannot be reconciled without reference to the spiritual, to the supernatural – to God, in fact. Edward Claflin says:

> We want to gaze at the impossible. We are hungry for surprise, astonishments. In short, we are looking for a true story, but one impossible to explain in all its complexity. When we discover that story we shall have found magic.[9]

It would be hard to find a more succinct expression of the longing that is spelled out in Ecclesiastes 3:11:

> God has made everything beautiful for its own time. He has planted eternity in the human heart, but even so, people cannot see the whole scope of God's work from beginning to end.

Our finite universe contains something bigger than itself; a box contains a box that it fits inside. It is impossible. And we want to gaze upon it. While Derren Brown believes that 'blind faith is something we need to grow out of', his shows vividly reveal that faith in what is unseen is alive and well in the twenty-first century marketplace. It is a marketplace we probably ought to be wandering about in, looking for these very spots marked 'Unknown God' and clearing our throats to speak . . .

Notes

[1] Mk. 9:24, NIV

[2] William of Occam was an English Franciscan friar in the fourteenth century who is best known for the principle known as Occam's razor: given two possible explanations for something, it is best to opt for the simpler one. For more on this see www.wikipedia.org/wiki/Ockham%27s_razor

[3] Edward Claflin and Jeff Sheridan, *Street Magic: An Illustrated History of Wandering Magicians and their Conjuring Arts* (Kaufman and Co., 1998), p. xiii (my italics)

[4] 'The Biggest Douche in the Universe', *Southpark* series 6, episode 615 (first broadcast in the UK on 27 November 2002). This episode is a no holds barred assault on the enormous popularity of shows like *Crossing Over with John Edward* in which a 'medium' loosely based on John Edward – and called John Edward – is exposed as a fraud and accused of horribly misleading vulnerable people. Ultimately, although at a cosmic level this reprehensible villain receives his comeuppance, the children are unable to convince anyone that such powers do not exist as, mysteriously, the desire to believe turns all their exposes into new demonstrations.

[5] 1 Sam. 28

[6] Karen Armstrong. *A Short History of Myth* (Canongate, 2005) p. 8–9

[7] *The Man with the Golden Gun* (dir. Guy Hamilton, MGM, 1974)

[8] Although the term 'Ouija board' is used generically, it is, in fact, a trade name of Parker Brothers. Ironically, the 'game' is manufactured in Salem, Massachusetts.

[9] Claflin and Sheridan, *Street Magic*, p. xiii

However you define God, and whether you believe in God or not, the world that we live in has been shaped by the universal human conviction that there is more to life than life itself; that there is a God-shaped hole at the centre of our universe.

Professor Robert Winston

4. Scary, Scary Night

Steve Couch

'They say this one has a surprise ending.'
(Elijah's mother, *Unbreakable*)

When writing *Unbreakable* (2000), his second major film,[1] M. Night Shyamalan couldn't resist a sly reference to the twist that made his previous movie, *The Sixth Sense* (1999), a runaway word-of-mouth success. *The Sixth Sense* made such an impression on the movie-going public that parodies and other references have cropped up as far afield as *The Simpsons*, the romantic comedy *50 First Dates* (2004), and even a *Comic Relief* version of BBC sitcom *One Foot In The Grave*. Certainly, the film is responsible for the common perception of a Shyamalan film as being structured to provide a last minute revelation, a clever twist that sheds new light on everything that has gone before, yet which is foreshadowed by numerous clues that only reveal themselves on a second or third viewing. To some extent, Shyamalan's later films have moved away from the last-gasp shock mode, but it is still true that all of his films contain major revelations which pull the rug out from under the audience's feet. If you haven't seen

The Sixth Sense (or, for that matter, any of Shyamalan's other work) you should know that this chapter contains major plot spoilers – if you don't want to know the respective twists and secrets, stop reading now.

Shyamalan's subsequent films have met with mixed reviews. The more hostile critics have accused his later efforts of failing to live up to *The Sixth Sense*, while others have acclaimed him as a distinctive and intelligent film-maker who stands out from many of his blockbuster-making contemporaries. Branded by some as 'the new Spielberg' (partly due to the recurring significance of family in his films), Shyamalan is perhaps better compared with a Hollywood great of a previous era. Like Alfred Hitchcock, Shyamalan has been accurately labelled a master of suspense (and, like his illustrious predecessor, also has a tendency to make cameo appearances in his own movies). Shyamalan himself has observed:

> The particular accent I speak in is suspense, so if two people are having a conversation, my mind will immediately go to: how do I do it in a way that creates a little ticking clock in you. Even if it's a romantic scene, or a scary scene, or an emotional scene, it's about defying expectations, even in the littlest moments.[2]

India's national newspaper *The Hindu* has described the air of suspense in Shyamalan's films as being, 'like an invisible animal in the room … something hidden … that decides to leave before it attacks.'[3] And this lingering sense of unease is coupled with the awareness that the unseen danger, the lurking mystery is not of this world. If Shyamalan's accent is suspense, his language is fear. When asked about his preoccupation with the fear of the unknown, Shyamalan responded, 'that *is* the definition of fear; fear is the unknown.'[4] And in each of his major movies, this fear of the unknown seems, on the surface at least, to be grounded in the world of the supernatural.

Suspense of Belief

From Cole (Haley Joel Osment) in *The Sixth Sense* admitting, 'I see dead people', to the blind Ivy Walker (Bryce Dallas Howard) in *The Village* (2004) facing the horror of 'those we do not speak of' in the woods, Shyamalan plays on our fear that there *is* something out there, and it means to do us harm. His next film, *Lady in the Water* is due for release in the summer of 2006, and (according to early reports) features Paul Giamatti as the superintendent of an apartment building who discovers a water-nymph living in the block's swimming pool and attempting to return to her home in the land of fairy tales. While it is always dangerous to comment on a film that hasn't yet been completed, it seems reasonable to assume that themes of the supernatural will once again be taking a central place.

But if we think of the supernatural as meaning ghosts, nymphs and inhuman creatures who live in the woods, then *The Sixth Sense* remains the most obvious example of Shyamalan's fascination with the subject. Doctor Malcolm Crowe (Bruce Willis) is an eminent child psychologist. Some months after a former patient breaks into his home and attempts to shoot him, Crowe starts meeting with a young boy, Cole Sear, who eventually reveals to Crowe that he frequently interacts with dead people. Sometimes they talk to him, and sometimes they attack him. In an attempt to protect himself, Cole has taken to stealing religious artefacts to put in the shrine-like tent that he uses as a hiding place in his bedroom. Crowe gradually becomes convinced that Cole's visions are real, and helps the youngster to make sense of his strange abilities, finally enabling him to realise his ambition to not 'be scared anymore'. Finally, Crowe discovers that he himself is one of Cole's ghostly visitors, the attempted shooting having been more successful than Crowe had realised. While the supernatural nature of the film is apparent from early on, the twist of Crowe's deceased status, although repeatedly hinted at throughout the film, works as a colossal bombshell for the first-time audience, delivering an enormous emotional impact while also resolving the outstanding plot issues.

So *The Sixth Sense* occupies classic spooky territory, and is elevated out of the genre's rank and file by virtue of Shyamalan's expert storytelling flair. Elsewhere in Shyamalan's major films, there is less of the supernatural than we might imagine. Granted, *Signs* (2002) gives us crop circles and malevolent aliens (if not supernatural, they can certainly claim to be other-worldly), and *The Village* at least has the pretence of beastly creatures – but significantly, they are revealed to be nothing more than pretence. The evil that the villagers flee turns out to be everyday fallen, sinful humanity. Similarly, this is the threat to David Dunn (Bruce Willis again) in *Unbreakable*, a film which offers us nothing more traditionally supernatural than an ordinary man who discovers that somehow he possesses exceptional powers, and a vocational calling as a superhero.

Fatalist Flaw

Where the supernatural really presents itself in Shyamalan's films is not so much with the trappings of spooks and creatures, but with the question of what type of universe we live in. Shyamalan presents us with an ordered universe, a directed universe. Repeatedly in his films, one character or another will express a fatalistic view along the lines that whatever is meant to happen, will happen. When Elijah Price (Samuel L. Jackson) is trying to convince David Dunn of his superheroic calling in *Unbreakable*, he suggests, 'that little bit of sadness in the mornings you spoke of, I think I know what it is: perhaps you're not doing what you're supposed to be doing.' Earlier we see Elijah's mother in flashback, telling her reclusive son, 'If that's what God has planned for you, that's what's going to happen. You can't hide from it sitting in a room.' In *Signs*, Graham Hess (Mel Gibson) is the minister of a church who has lost his faith after the death of his wife in a motoring accident. Both the victim and the other driver separately tell the minister, 'it was meant to be'. And in the final dramatic moments of the film, events conspire in such a way that Graham finally regains his faith in God, and particularly in God's ability to work events together for good. In *The Village*, an impromptu elders' debate about whether to allow Ivy Walker to fetch medicine from the town is settled by August Nicholson (Brendan Gleeson). The villagers live secretly, hidden away from the evils of the modern world. The elders fear that if Ivy gives away their secret, the very existence of the community could be at risk, but August argues that she should go, reasoning that 'if this place is of worth, it will stand'.

All of those remarks belong only in a world where events are not random, where some force – call it destiny or call it God – shapes events; a supernatural world. Ironically, it is the most obviously supernatural of Shyamalan's films, *The Sixth Sense*, which provides

the greatest contrast to this tendency. While there is
clearly a supernatural element – large numbers of
ghosts, including one of the two central protagonists
– it seems to be a world where God is either missing or
disinterested. The ghosts themselves are portrayed as
tortured souls who have died leaving things undone,
things that prevent them from finding rest. Cole tells
us that, 'they don't see each other, they only see what
they want to see. They don't know they're dead.' These
are lost souls who have fallen between the cracks in
a universe where nobody is looking for them. God's
absence is reinforced both by the inadequacy of Cole's
stolen icons to help him, and by the words of his
mother, who says, 'I've been praying. I guess I've not
been praying right. I guess we're just going to have to
answer each other's prayers.'

In *The Village*, the settlement has the air of a simple
but sincere religious community. We see simple rituals
– a funeral, a wedding – and communal meals where
words are spoken with the air of liturgy, yet there is
very little mention of God. One girl says to her newly
engaged sister, 'God bless you and your life together,'
and the elders' oath to never return to the town is
described as 'sacred', but there is little of substance to
back up the view that this is a community which places
any great emphasis on God. There may be a belief in
goodness and wickedness – the community exists as a
response to the crime and murders that have blighted
the lives of the elders in the outside world – and the
aforementioned confidence that the community will
endure if it is of worth, but we are presented with no
rationale as to why this should be so.

Your Will be Done

Only in *Signs* do we move explicitly from the idea of a purposeful universe of design to the question of the designer. Less than five minutes into the film, Graham discovers his young son Morgan (Rory Culkin), fascinated by the complex crop circle patterns that the aliens have created in the Hess cornfields. Without taking his eyes from the patterns, Morgan says, 'I think God did it.' Graham doesn't reply, and we subsequently realise that any contemplation of God is simply too painful for the recently-widowed former man of the cloth. The fact that when the line is spoken neither Graham nor the audience has actually seen the crop patterns adds to the weight of the line, and its effect in presenting God front and centre of our minds as the rest of the film unfolds.

What follows is a fascinating portrayal of a faith that has crumbled under the pressure of intense grief, and which is rekindled only through another harrowing experience of potential loss. A few minutes after Morgan's theological musings, policewoman Paski (Cherry Jones) and Graham are discussing whether the stalks have been broken by hand or by machine. 'What kind of machine can bend a stalk of corn over without breaking it?' she asks. There is a sense that this reflects the journey that Graham is on: he has been bent over and laid low, and yet by the end of the film we realise that even the death of his wife has not completely broken either the man or his faith. There are parallels with Isaiah 42:3 ('A bruised reed he will not break, and a smouldering wick he will not snuff out' (NIV)) or with 1 Corinthians 10:13 ('God is faithful. He will keep the temptation from becoming so strong that you can't stand up against it'). Such a reading invites *Signs* to be viewed as the story of God's plan to revive Graham's faith. There are a number of subtle visual cues to reinforce the religious perspective of the film – for example, an aerial shot of the neighbourhood, seen as the Hess family drives into town, passes over a cross shaped concrete patio and a local church. Although Graham tells Merrill (Joachin Phoenix) that his wife Colleen's final words were meaningless, nothing more than the random firing of nerve endings in her mind, when we subsequently see the scene in flashback, Colleen's prescience of the alien attack makes her remarks also interpretable as an advance-notice message from God.

Signs and Wondering

The thematically pivotal scene of the film sees Graham and Merrill on the sofa, discussing the breaking news that alien space ships have been sighted. Merrill asks Graham for some hope, to which Graham replies that the world can be divided into two groups of people: those who put whatever happens down to coincidence and luck, and those who see it as a sign that there is someone out there watching over them. For the first group, the discovery of aliens is worrying. It could be good news; it could be bad, but whichever it is, they know that they will face it on their own, which makes them fearful. For the second group, they know that whatever happens with the aliens, there will be someone there to help them – a knowledge which fills them with hope. Graham's words are comforting to Merrill, but they are just words. When pushed, Graham places himself firmly in the 'just luck' camp. 'There is no one watching out for us,' he tells Merrill. 'We are all on our own.' The film asks us which group we place ourselves in, and uses Graham's journey back to faith to challenge those who dismiss the concept of the universe having either a grand design or a grand designer.

The depth of Graham's rejection of God is shown in a later scene where the Hess family have barricaded themselves into their farmhouse. Morgan wants to pray before a meal, and Graham overreacts, harshly stating that he is 'not wasting one more minute of my life on prayer, not one more minute'. Later, as Morgan suffers an asthma attack, Graham turns on God: 'Don't do this to me again, not again. I hate you, I hate you.'

But by the end of the film, Graham sees how everything – Colleen's mysterious dying words, Merrill's youthful prowess with a baseball bat, Morgan's asthma and even daughter Bo's (Abilgail Breslin) inexplicable inability to finish a glass of water – has all combined to preserve Morgan's life. As Graham – and the audience – waits to see whether Morgan has survived his ordeal, Graham says, 'That's why he had asthma. It can't be luck. His lungs were closed – no poison got in.' Morgan revives and asks, 'Dad, what happened? Did someone save me?' to which his father replies, 'Yeah, I think someone did.'

I Want to be Free

But there is always a danger of reading our own theological perspective onto someone else's art. While promoting *Signs*, Shyamalan himself commented that, 'I'm not very religious … I believe in a presence or God, just not in religion.'[5] While *Signs* is undoubtedly the story of a man regaining his faith, we should not read too much into the fact that in this case Shyamalan has chosen the Christian faith for his protagonist.

Shyamalan himself was born in Pondicherry, India, but raised in the affluent suburbs of Philadelphia. His parents sent him to a Christian school (for the school's strict discipline) but brought him up as a Hindu. Unsurprisingly with this cosmopolitan background, Shyamalan seems to have a syncretistic approach to matters of faith, doubting whether any one religion has all of the answers. But he has also commented that his scepticism is akin to Houdini's – 'Please show me, but don't fool me'[6] – including a sincere desire to know the truth. What is undeniable is that his movies, individually and collectively, point to the conclusion that there is something out there.

There may be something out there, but what difference does that actually make to us? For Shyamalan, the presence of a designer also brings with it the problem of free will. He has his characters make decisive choices, yet he also presents us with a universe where whatever is meant to happen will happen. This raises the long standing Christian tension between belief in a loving, sovereign God and belief in a God who has given men and women free will and the ability to determine their own actions. Both views can be supported from the Bible, yet how can they be reconciled? To put it another way, if God has decreed that little Morgan Hess is going to survive the alien poison attack, does Merrill have a choice about whether or not he picks up the baseball bat? If Merrill chooses not to 'swing away', will Morgan still survive? If not, what does that say about God's so-called sovereignty?

The tension between these two conflicting theological concepts has long been at the heart of orthodox Christian faith. Two distinct theological branches, Calvinism and Arminianism, represent the two extremes of the argument, with the third perspective of Compatibilism occupying the middle ground.

Calvinism would argue that free will is an illusion. God has chosen the elect – those he will save – and the elect are the elect are the elect. If your name is on the roll of glory in heaven then there is nothing you can do about it, sooner or later you are going to turn to God. The Arminian counters by asking how the non-elect can be held responsible for their sins when there was no possibility for them to repent and put their faith in God anyway? If there is no free will, how can anyone be held morally accountable for things they had no control over?

Arminianism suggests that God calls everyone and that he helps us to make wise choices in accordance to his plans for us. However, we have the ability to choose whether or not to respond to God's prompting. God may want us to repent and put our faith in Jesus, but it is up to us whether or not we do so. By this way of thinking, God doesn't decide who will put their faith in him and who won't, but he knows in advance the result of the free choices that each of us will make. The Calvinist would respond that this strips God of his sovereignty, reducing him to a hopeful suitor waiting on tenterhooks for our answer to his proposal. In essence, the Calvinist would accuse the Arminian of elevating the human will over and above God's will, setting ourselves in the place of the supreme power in the universe.[7]

The Compatibilist position tries to hold together these two contradictory strands. God's sovereignty is reasserted: God's will does reign supreme in the world; but it does so by working through the complex web of freely made human decisions. Because our actions are the result of free choice, we are rightly held accountable for them, and we can only be saved through the exercise of God's grace and mercy. Quite how these two are reconciled is frankly a mystery, and perhaps the Shyamalan-like twist in the tale of our lives will be when we meet God in heaven and finally understand how this paradox actually fits together.

Extending Hope

It is worth pointing out that the above theological discussion is concerned primarily with the salvation of individual men and women, rather than with whether or not God has preordained every aspect of life on earth. Most Calvinists would not say that God has decreed whether you should catch the 8.15 a.m. or the 8.30 a.m. train, or whether you should eat egg sandwiches or cheese for your lunch. We do know that God's will for his people (whatever we believe about how those people are chosen) is that they will be reconciled to him and to be presented perfect in Jesus on the last day.[8] This is the life that God made men and women for, and this is the ultimate expression of his will. Whatever our perspective on the degree of freedom our friends and neighbours may have in responding to that invitation, part of our responsibility is to present them with the opportunity, to gently and sensitively put the claims of Jesus before them and to pray that somewhere between them and God there will be a meeting of wills and a submission to God's rightful authority in all of our lives.

In the world of Shyamalan's films, the supernatural is undeniably real. The world is not reduced to what we can see with our eyes or measure scientifically.

There is a higher power at work, and that power has our best interests at heart. Christians would want to take the argument a stage further: God isn't just a cosmic force of destiny, he is a relational, loving God who takes charge of his world and weaves together the whole story of human history, with all of the freely made choices and decisions, and works out his plan to reconcile his people to him. While Hollywood typically represents the existence of the supernatural as a reason to be afraid, Christians would echo Graham Hess in stating that for those who believe in more than just coincidence, the knowledge that we are not alone fills us with hope. In *Unbreakable*, super-villain Elijah Price tells David Dunn that the scariest thing is 'to not know your place in the world, to not know why you're here'. The Christian faith offers an answer to that uncertainty, and offers the reassurance of a superhero who faces death on our behalf and comes out the other side triumphant. We may not see dead people, but we know a man who was dead and is now alive, and who is on our side. In a world where fear and terror are increasingly prevalent, that message of hope is a powerful one indeed.

Notes

[1] Before his big breakthrough with *The Sixth Sense*, Shyamalan had already written and directed two other films which failed to make any significant impression. *Praying With Anger* (1992) starred Shyamalan as an Americanised Indian who experiences culture shock on returning to India on a college exchange programme. *Wide Awake* (1998) is a light family comedy featuring a ten-year-old boy searching for God after the death of his grandfather, and starring comic actress Rosie O'Donnell as a sports-loving nun who tries to help him. It is possibly most notable for being the only

Shyamalan-directed film in which he doesn't appear on screen. Shyamalan also wrote the screenplay to the decidedly unspooky hit comedy *Stuart Little* (1999).

[2] M. Night Shyamalan, interviewed by Alana Lee – www.bbc.co.uk/films/2004/08/11/m_night_shyamalan_the_village_interview.shtml

[3] Uma Mahadevan-Dasgupta, 'In Nuance Lies His Strength', *The Hindu*, 6 September 2002

[4] M. Night Shyamalan, interviewed by Alana Lee

[5] M. Night Shyamalan, quoted in Ian Freer, 'Field of Screams', *Empire*, October 2002, p. 58

[6] M. Night Shyamalan, quoted in Wilson Morales, 'The Man With A Vision: An interview with M. Night Shyamalan', Blackfilm.com (August 2002) – blackfilm.com/20020823/features/mnightshyamalan.shtml

[7] The Calvinist, Arminian and Compatibilist views all fall within the realm of legitimate orthodox Christian theology. A more recent theological development is the 'Openness of God' theology, which argues that not only does God not preordain what will happen, but that he doesn't foreknow it either – in effect, he sits and waits to find out what is going to happen with the rest of us. For many evangelicals, this watering down of God's sovereignty amounts to outright heresy.

[8] Col. 1:28

It's natural, even healthy, to question the world we're presented. You might say it's only human.

Dr Merrick in the film *The Island*

5. Putting Adult Ways Behind Us

Tony Watkins

The publishing phenomenon of the last decade has been the new-found respectability of children's fiction. After years of being sidelined within the publishing world, it is suddenly centre stage. No longer are adults looking down their grown-up noses at 'kids' stuff'. We'll happily sit on a train reading J.K. Rowling, Philip Pullman, G.P. Taylor, Mark Haddon, Garth Nix, perhaps even, as a result of the success of *The Chronicles of Narnia* in cinemas, C.S. Lewis. There is still an element of adult snobbery, though. Publishers now tend to produce 'adult editions' so that the books at least *look* grown up. And we like to describe these books in a way that doesn't smack of a lack of sophistication: we don't care to refer to them as *children's* fiction but as *crossover* fiction. The event that best symbolised this big change in publishing was Philip Pullman winning the 2001 Whitbread Award for *The Amber Spyglass*. He was the first winner of the Whitbread Children's Book Award to win the overall prize.

Interestingly, the books which have become crossover bestsellers are predominantly fantasy literature with strong elements of the supernatural or magic. Of my list of authors above, only Mark Haddon is not writing in this genre. What is particularly curious is that fantasy has often been rather looked down upon by the literary establishment. Writing in 1996, Lucie Armitt reflected that:

> If you place 'fantastic' in a literary context . . . suddenly we have a problem. Suddenly it is something dubious, embarrassing. . . . Suddenly we need to justify our interest in it . . . its presumed association with the formulaic inevitably attracts two negative [views] . . . escapism and pulp fiction.[1]

Peter Hunt commented on this passage in 2001: 'Worse, it is associated with that still-marginalised form, children's literature.'[2] As we have already noted, much has changed in the respectability of children's literature even in the few years since then, but the association of fantasy with children's (or crossover) literature is still strong, and it is almost as though two maligned areas of literature have found respectability by being combined. But this change has not happened as a result of them combining – there has been fantasy for both adults and children for a very long time. We will briefly survey some of the major contributors to this field, and then see if the common threads help us to understand why children's fiction focusing on the supernatural now has such widespread appeal.

J.K. Rowling

It was, of course, Harry Potter who blazed the trail on his broomstick. Until two years before Pullman's Whitbread triumph, it had been inconceivable that a children's book could ever win such a prestigious award. J.K. Rowling's *Harry Potter and the Prisoner of Azkaban* caused a stir by being seriously considered for the 1999 Award, finally losing out (apparently on a five to four split among the judges) to Seamus Heaney's magnificent translation of *Beowulf*. Surprisingly, in all the controversy there was very little comment on the fact that both front runners were fantasies. In 2005, sales of *Harry Potter and the Half-Blood Prince* broke all records. An estimated ten million copies were sold worldwide within the first twenty-four hours after going on sale, over two million of them in the UK. That's more than Dan Brown's *The Da Vinci Code* sold in a year. The previous five books had already sold over 250 million copies worldwide, helping forty-year-old Jo Rowling to become a billionaire.

Despite being the world's most successful author – perhaps partly because of it – she has some very outspoken critics. A.S. Byatt, for example, wrote in the *New York Times:*

> Ms Rowling's magic world has no place for the numinous. It is written for people whose imaginative lives are confined to TV cartoons and the exaggerated (more exciting, not threatening) mirror-worlds of soaps, reality TV and celebrity gossip. . . . Ms Rowling, I think, speaks to an adult generation, that hasn't known and doesn't care about mystery.[3]

These comments are typical of critics who feel that they represent some high culture which is in a different league from populist authors like Rowling. She has been accused of being derivative, but others reply that this is a pejorative way of saying that she has allusions to plenty of other children's literature – so many, and handled so skilfully, in fact, that it is a mark of her intelligence as a writer. Children's literature specialist Peter Hunt says that her success 'might, at least initially, derive from the fact that . . . she was *not* following a formula for what a children's book should be like: rather, she seems to have been tracing echoes.'[4] The further we get in the series, the more we see just how carefully intricate her plotting is, yet this does not overwhelm the sense of pace and drama. The stories are full of excitement and deal with a very broad emotional range.

Some Christians, however, have attacked her – sometimes very aggressively – for writing about wizards, witches and magic. Such stories, they argue, attract impressionable children into the real-life world of the occult. Others claim that there is no clear distinction between good and evil – the heroes succeed by rebelling against authority, and by lying and deception. However, many Christians retort that the heroes are realistically imperfect, but that there is a very clear fundamental distinction between good and evil. Jerram Barrs, for example, sees this in:

> Both the appalling destructiveness of evil to human life and the beneficial fruit of treating people with justice, kindness, mercy, faithfulness, and integrity. It is particularly significant that the books recognise that goodness and faithfulness in relationships have a cost. Virtue is rewarded primarily in terms of character development and the increasing depths of relationships among the characters, rather than through the attainment of popularity or success.[5]

There is no shortage of big themes in *Harry Potter* books – adolescence, ambition, power, relationships, and, especially, death.

Philip Pullman

The next biggest in terms of sales is Philip Pullman, best known for *His Dark Materials* – a fantasy trilogy comprising *Northern Lights, The Subtle Knife* and *The Amber Spyglass* – though he is the author of over twenty other books. Unlike Rowling, however, he is widely respected in the literary establishment. As well as the Whitbread Award, Pullman has won a number of others including the world's most prestigious prize for children's fiction, the Astrid Lindgren Memorial Award in 2005.[6] In the BBC's 2003 poll of Britain's favourite book, *The Big Read, His Dark Materials* came in at third place – the highest position for any living author.[7]

A key element in the appeal of *His Dark Materials* is the dazzling breadth of Pullman's story and its complexity. He weaves into the narrative powerful themes and big philosophical issues which engage any active mind: growing up, wisdom, separation and death, misuse of authority, freedom, responsibility, consciousness and God. Millicent Lenz says:

> *His Dark Materials* interweaves an engrossing, breath-taking adventure story with a deeply felt examination of existential questions, such as Mrs Coulter's anguished plea to know whether God is, as Nietzsche asserted, 'dead', or why, if he still lives, he has grown mute. In his bold willingness to take on this and other 'big' questions . . . Pullman differs from more timid contemporary writers.[8]

Pullman's angle on God has, predictably, enraged many Christians – especially because of his outspoken antipathy towards Christianity (and religion in general) in interviews. In one he candidly admitted, 'My books are about killing God,'[9] and in another he stated, 'I'm

trying to undermine the basis of Christian belief.'[10] In
The Amber Spyglass, Pullman portrays God as merely
the first angel, who tricked those who came later into
thinking that he had created them. Eventually, Pullman
kills his God off, with the heroes of the book accidentally
performing a mercy-killing for a being who has lived
beyond his natural lifespan. But, Pullman says, we still
need the idea of heaven:

> . . . a sense of rightness and goodness and connectedness
> and meaning . . . But because there ain't no elsewhere,
> that has got to exist in the only place we know about
> for sure which is this earth, and we've got to make our
> world as good as we possibly can for one another and
> for our descendants. That's what I mean by a republic of
> heaven.[11]

Death is a hugely important theme for Pullman,
too. The heroes of *His Dark Materials* provide a way
out of the prison camp of the world of the dead, so
that the ghosts – which are still physical, though
insubstantial – can go free and dissolve back into the
universe.

Garth Nix

Garth Nix is a rising star in the world of crossover
fiction, though his *Keys to the Kingdom* series (still in
progress) seems to appeal to adults less than the *Old
Kingdom* trilogy – *Sabriel, Lirael* and *Abhorsen* – which
brought him to prominence. Nix is an Australian who
has been hailed by some as the successor to Philip
Pullman. Since Pullman continues to be a publishing
sensation, that seems a little hasty. But Nix is a great
writer – praised by Pullman himself.

The *Old Kingdom* trilogy is set in a fabulously curious world in which the very ordinary country of Ancelstierre (evocative of early twentieth-century Britain) borders the deeply magical and dangerous Old Kingdom. The two realms are divided by an ancient great wall and a 'perimeter zone' which has strong echoes of a World War I defensive line. These constitute a feeble defence against terrible dead beings and Free Magic creatures which bring terror throughout the Old Kingdom, and, at times, in the area around the perimeter zone.

The story begins with Sabriel nearing the end of schooldays in Ancelstierre. When her father goes missing she must return to the Old Kingdom to find him. But she knows that her search will take her into Death, for her father is the Abhorsen – the one who struggles with the Dead, binds them and sends them deep into Death, past all nine gates through which the icy river of Death flows.

Of course, this is all far removed from the real world, but Nix – like Pullman – thinks that 'the best fantasy is very firmly grounded in reality . . . It takes [readers] someplace else. But in that other world that they are taken to, all sorts of human experiences can be addressed – life, death, love, and tragedy.' Nix's handling of these themes is what makes his writing so emotionally engaging – it makes it feel very real.

G.P. Taylor

Life for Graham Taylor has taken some interesting twists and turns. Once a drug-fuelled punk working in the music industry, he was on the road to self-destruction. Until God turned him around, after which he became a social worker then a policeman. His police career ended after he was viciously beaten, but he was already on the way to being a vicar. Now, of course, G.P. Taylor is a best-selling author and says, 'I just feel that I've found where God wants me to be.'

Taylor's fame has come as a complete – and sometimes uncomfortable – surprise to him. He sold his motorbike to pay for the printing of his first novel, *Shadowmancer,* but once Faber & Faber took it up, there was no looking back. Universal Pictures bought the film rights and a Manga comic version has been published recently. Now Taylor's third novel *Tersias* is giving readers more of the same mix of a grim eighteenth-century setting and supernatural goings on that we're familiar with from *Shadowmancer* and *Wormwood.*

Some Christian readers have praised Taylor for writing powerful fantasy literature which has a thoroughly Christian worldview underpinning it. They see his work as having much more in common with Lewis or Tolkien than with Pullman or Rowling. There certainly are strong connections with Lewis in that both very deliberately use Christian ideas or values within their books. But Taylor's books feel worlds apart from all those authors in many ways. He's much closer to Garth Nix in his dark and at times gruesome portrayal of the supernatural. His rather macabre tales have brought attacks from some Christians who were initially positive about them. Focus on the Family said that *Wormwood* has a 'disturbing spiritual dynamic'.[12] The evil people and beings in *Tersias* really are very evil and are extremely powerful. The heroes, by contrast, are not powerfully good, but are themselves villains. Jonah Ketch is a would-be-highwayman and Magnus Malachi is a cruel, unscrupulous magician. They seem to have neither the abilities nor the moral fibre necessary to defeat their adversaries.

However, it seems to me that this is a good reflection of the Bible's view of human nature which sees us all as deeply flawed – not just a little flaky around the edges, but slaves to sin. *Tersias* also agrees with the Bible that true redemption only comes through an encounter with God's grace (though God is hinted at without being explicitly included). However dark they get, Taylor's books rest very firmly on the Christian conviction that God (and therefore good) is ultimately the strongest supernatural power there is.

Fictional Attraction

So, what is the appeal to adults of reading crossover fiction? It's not that the world is a simpler, more easily negotiated place in these books. In some cases it is quite the opposite. Garth Nix's world of the Old Kingdom is a terrifying place, for example – not easily negotiated at all. The moral ambiguity of some of G.P. Taylor's characters makes them anything but simple, and the multiple worlds within Pullman's *His Dark Materials* are sophisticated and, at times, perplexing. Rowling, too, has levels of complexity which readers often overlook at first, carried along as they are by the exciting narrative. Indeed, the simpler children's fiction doesn't seem to hold much appeal for adults (maybe not much for children either, given the enormous popularity of these authors). It feels too much like 'kid's stuff' to be satisfying.

Philip Pullman has characteristically strong views on this subject. 'There are some themes, some subjects, too large for adult fiction,' he declared in his Carnegie Medal acceptance speech. 'They can only be dealt with adequately in a children's book.'[13] The reason for this is that children's fiction is still about telling good stories. Pullman criticises much adult fiction as being too clever for its own good, with the story coming a poor second to the author's literary posing. Adults, like children, are hungry for stories. Stories are one of the key ways in which we make sense of the world. Daniel Taylor says that:

> Stories link past, present and future in a way that tells us where we have been (even before we were born), where we are, and where we are going. . . . Our stories teach us that there is a place for us, that we fit. They suggest to us that our lives can have a plot. Stories turn mere chronology, one thing after another, into the purposeful action of plot, and thereby into meaning. . . . Stories are the single best way humans have for accounting for our experience.[14]

So stories help us to learn wisdom and morality. As Pullman said:

> Stories are vital. Stories never fail us because, as Isaac Bashevis Singer says, 'events never grow stale.' There's more wisdom in a story than in volumes of philosophy. So when we discover that some of the best children's books tackle life's big issues in the context of great tales, we lap them up. We'd rather engage with a gripping story that deals with big issues than read stuffy grown up books about the same issues. All stories teach, whether the storyteller intends them to or not. They teach the world we create. They teach the morality we live by. They teach it much more effectively than moral precepts and instructions.[15]

Changing Writing, Changing Readers or Changing World?

There would seem only three possible explanations for the rise in crossover fiction within the last decade: the nature of the writing has changed, the nature of the readers has changed, or something has changed in the world in which we live.

I am not at all sure that crossover fiction represents a substantial change in what is written. Today's writers are not, in general, better than their predecessors. Pullman is without doubt one of the most outstanding authors of his generation, but there have been truly great writers of children's fantasy literature before – Ursula Le Guin and her *Earthsea* cycle, for example.[16] Rowling has not sold an unprecedented number of books because she is a great *writer*; but because she is a great *storyteller* whose stories have caught people's imaginations. While the writing of all these authors is fresh and vivid, none of them has pioneered a notable change in the style of writing; rather, they continue to develop, in their different ways, approaches that have already been tried and tested. Any changes in the content of what is written, however, may well be reflective of changes within society as a whole – particularly at a worldview level.

Have people changed much? Clearly, spending habits change constantly and book sales have been generally increasing for some time. More importantly, trends in buying books (more than most products) are strongly influenced by psychological and sociological factors. Again, this is bound up with broader cultural shifts.

So, what has changed at a cultural level? Maybe it is nothing more than society reaching what Malcolm Gladwell calls a tipping point[17] – the combined effect of word of mouth, clever marketing, and all kinds of other apparently insignificant factors. But there are still strong psychological factors involved in big changes. There needs to be some kind of readiness or receptivity in the culture for a new idea or a new trend.

The clues might be in what these writers have in common. First, and most obviously, they are all about alternative worlds, whether they are parallel to our normal world (the wizard world of *Harry Potter;* the many worlds in *His Dark Materials)* or an alternative vision of our world into which magic breaks in (Taylor's magical eighteenth century). Some people dismiss 'alternative world fiction' as escapist, but all fiction is escapist in that sense, since even a 'normal' world in fiction is still invented – it is not *our* world. Could it be that various changes in the outlook of our society, coupled with rising fears about where our world might be heading, have made us eager to escape into alternative worlds in which there is discernible good and evil, and in which we might find some hope for the future? Could it be that we go to crossover fantasy literature because there we find stories which help us to deal with the reality in which we live? As Peter Hunt says, 'the one thing that can rarely be said of fantasy is that it has nothing to do with reality'.[18] Jill Paton Walsh argues that fantasy helps us to think about our world in ways which other fiction cannot:

> A work of fantasy compels the reader into a metaphorical state of mind. A work of realism, on the other hand, permits very literal-minded readings. . . . Even worse, it is possible to read a realistic book as though it were not fiction at all.[19]

Second, these alternative worlds are full of the supernatural, whether it be magic, spirits, or the dead.

Even Pullman's trilogy is full of the supernatural in some sense, despite the fact that he doesn't believe in it. Our postmodern world has put spirituality back on the agenda. The out-and-out materialism (belief that only the physical world is real) of people like Richard Dawkins still appeals to some, but there are many who profoundly disagree, whether or not they are religious in any traditional sense. In a post-Christian – and partly post-materialist – culture, people are very happy to explore all kinds of supernatural possibilities in books and elsewhere.

Third, these stories are all about the classic struggle between good and evil. This is highly significant, I believe. We live in a world where people are less and less sure of the difference. Some time ago, I got into discussion with a children's author on a train. He was adamant that there is no good or evil. He totally rejected the categories. But most people intuitively know that such an approach to life is not good enough. Does this literature help people to feel as well as understand that the categories really do mean something?

One of the reasons this literature is so engaging is that good and evil are not presented in simplistic black and white terms – we have to wrestle with them. These authors' books all feature clearly discernible evil, and all unreservedly stress the good of strong moral values (courage, integrity, compassion, self-sacrifice, and many more), but the characters are often a mix of good and bad. Ursula Le Guin believes that, 'Fantasy is the natural, the appropriate language for the recounting of the spiritual journey and the struggle of good and evil in the soul.'[20] The world of the *Old Kingdom* trilogy contains terrifying evil, but the protagonists have a deep sense of responsibility to confront it, despite their fears, insecurities and lack of resources. They must try to do *something*, regardless of the personal cost even if the chances of success seem slim; to do nothing in the face of evil means certain defeat. It's an attitude which makes them inspiring heroes for our real world where evil within society is more complex, harder to deal with, but which must be resisted nevertheless. Nix says, 'where good does triumph it's never without cost. I think real life is like that, too. You generally have to pay for the triumph or make great sacrifices to conquer evil.'[21]

Fourth, there is a preoccupation with death. Children who have lost their parents are a familiar feature of children's fantasy literature, but all these writers deal with death in far broader terms than orphans coping with their situations in life. Geordie Greig writes:

> Death is the key to understanding J.K. Rowling. Her greatest fear – and she is completely unhesitant about this – is of someone she loves dying. [Rowling says] 'My books are largely about death. They open with the death of Harry's parents. There is Voldemort's obsession with conquering death and his quest for immortality at any price, the goal of anyone with magic. I so understand why Voldemort wants to conquer death. We're all frightened of it.'[22]

We live in a world in which death is the last taboo. We have pushed it out of our homes and sanitised it by approaching it only within the confines of clinical environments. We have pushed it away by developing such sophisticated technology that we find ourselves surprised and feeling betrayed when someone dies at what we consider to be an early age. In this context, fantasy literature helps us to face it and reminds us that death need not be the end.

Responding

These four themes are enormously important – and Christians have a distinctive perspective on them. We do believe in an alternative world, one that can be experienced now and will be entered fully at death – an event that need not cause us to fear because one who is perfectly good has supernaturally entered our world to bring about, in his own self-sacrifice, the ultimate defeat of evil. This is fact, not fantasy, but the resonances with the world of crossover fantasy literature are powerful enough that we should be working hard at understanding it and learning to speak its language into the world around us.

Tolkien believed that fantasy is 'not a lower but a higher form of Art, indeed the most nearly pure form, and so (when achieved) the most potent'.[23] Ursula Le Guin felt similarly:

> For fantasy is true, of course. It isn't factual, but it is true. Children know that. Adults know it too, and that is precisely why many of them are afraid of fantasy. They know that its truth challenges, even threatens, all that is false, all that is phoney, unnecessary, and trivial in the life they have let themselves be forced into living. They are afraid of dragons because they are afraid of freedom.[24]

Notes

[1] Lucie Armitt, *Theorising the Fantastic* (Arnold, 1996), quoted in Peter Hunt and Millicent Lenz, *Alternative Worlds in Fantasy Fiction* (Continuum, 2001), p. 1–2

[2] Peter Hunt in Hunt and Lenz, *Alternative Worlds in Fantasy Fiction*, p. 2

3 A.S. Byatt, 'Harry Potter and the Childish Adult', *New York Times*, 7 July 2003

4 Peter Hunt, *Children's Literature* (Blackwell, 2001), p. 122

5 Jerram Barrs, 'J.K. Rowling and Harry Potter', *Bethinking* – www.bethinking.org/viewall.php?ID=84

6 Shared with Japanese illustrator Ryoji Arai. For more information, see www.alma.se

7 In first and second place were J.R.R Tolkien's *The Lord of the Rings* and Jane Austen's *Pride and Prejudice* which consistently came top of other polls – even before the films of *The Lord of the Rings* came out

8 Millicent Lenz, 'Philip Pullman' in Hunt and Lenz, *Alternative Worlds in Fantasy Fiction*, pp. 122–123

9 Steve Meacham, 'The shed where God died', *Sidney Morning Herald*, 13 December 2003

10 Alona Wartofsky, 'The Last Word', *Washington Post*, 19 February 2001

11 Tony Watkins, 'Interview with Philip Pullman', *CultureWatch* – www.damaris.org/content/content.php?type=5&id=369

12 Julie Smithouser, 'G.P. Taylor's Wormwood', *Plugged In Online* – pluggedinonline.com/articles/a0001897.cfm

13 Philip Pullman, Carnegie Medal Acceptance Speech – www.randomhouse.com/features/pullman/philippullman/speech.html

14 Daniel Taylor, *The Healing Power of Worldviews: Creating Yourself Through the Stories of Your Life* (Gill & Macmillan, 1996), p. 140, quoted in Brian Godawa, *Hollywood Worldviews: Watching Films with Wisdom and Discernment* (IVP, 2002), p. 33

15 Pullman, Carnegie Medal Acceptance Speech

16 The original trilogy consists of *A Wizard of Earthsea* (1968), *The Tombs of Atuan* (1971) and *The Farthest Shore* (1972). In 1990 she added *Tehanu: The Last Book of Earthsea*

17 Malcolm Gladwell, *The Tipping Point: How Little Things Can Make a Big Difference* (Abacus, 2002)

18 Peter Hunt in Hunt and Lenz, *Alternative Worlds in Fantasy Fiction*, p. 2

[19] Jill Paton Walsh, quoted in Hunt, *Children's Literature*, p. 270

[20] Ursula K. Le Guin, *The Language of the Night: Essays on Fantasy and Science Fiction*, second edition (HarperCollins, 1992), p. 64

[21] 'An Interview with Garth Nix', *Harper Teen* – www.harperteen.com/global_scripts/product_catalog/book_xml.asp?isbn=0060278234&tc=ai

[22] Geordie Greig, 'There would be so much to tell her . . .', *Daily Telegraph*, 10 January 2006 – www.telegraph.co.uk/arts/main.jhtml?xml=/arts/2006/01/10/ftpotter10.xml

[23] J.R.R. Tolkien, 'On Fairy Stories' in *Tree and Leaf* (Allen and Unwin, 1964), p. 70

[24] Ursula K. Le Guin, *The Language of the Night*, p. 40

Whether it's religion or my own scepticism, we all notice what supports our beliefs and we disregard the rest.

Derren Brown in *Messiah*

6. Demons on Trial?

Rebecca Ward

'I don't know if I believe in demons ... I'm not asking you to believe in demons ... But is it possible?'
Erin Bruner summing up the defence case in
'The People v Father Richard Moore'

Do demons exist? Can they take possession of a person? For people who believe the stories contained in the Bible, these questions must be answered with a 'Yes'. But what if you don't believe? It seems most people know a ghost story – although it always seems to have happened to a friend of a friend. But seeing a dark shadow one night and being possessed by a demon are two very different things. *The Exorcism of Emily Rose* is a disturbing film which looks at these issues and raises very controversial questions for those who are Christians as well as those who aren't. But looking at it positively, it opens up so many issues relating to the supernatural and the reality of evil, and it may give us some useful pointers to help us to talk to our friends about these things. Director Scott Derrickson says:

I really just wanted to make a film that was going to provoke the mainstream audience to ask themselves what they believe, and cause them to come away from the film provoked to think about and discuss spiritual matters and spiritual issues that I think are profoundly important.[1]

The Exposition of Emily Rose

The Exorcism of Emily Rose follows the trial of a Catholic priest charged with negligent homicide following the death of a teenage girl. The circumstances surrounding her death are highly controversial. Emily Rose (Jennifer Carpenter) had left her family home to start college. Alone one night in her student dorm, she started to experience what appear to be terrifying hallucinations and invisible physical attack, after which she fell unconscious. She was admitted to hospital and prescribed medication – a drug called Gambutrol, used to treat epilepsy. However, her symptoms became increasingly severe and occurred more frequently, and eventually she turned to her family priest Father Richard Moore (Tom Wilkinson) for help.

Father Moore believed Emily to be demon possessed and, with her consent, performed an exorcism. The priest's actions were unsuccessful, and Emily's symptoms continued to worsen. Her violent outbreaks and aversion to food resulted in her death shortly afterwards. The cause of death was determined to be a gradual shutdown of bodily function – the cumulative effect of several physical traumas exacerbated by malnutrition.

One important piece of information to note is about the drug Gambutrol. In the film it is said to have a cumulative effect – that is, if taken consistently, the effectiveness increases over time. The doctors believed that the drug would eventually manage Emily's symptoms. But Father Moore believed that the drug had locked Emily in her possessed state and made the exorcism ineffective. Consequently, he persuaded Emily to stop taking it. If the doctors were right that Emily was suffering from a psychotic epileptic disorder, then Father Moore's advice and action led directly to her death. If, however, she really was demon possessed, then he had done everything possible to heal her.

The Exorcism of Emily Rose sees a court of law deciding whether or not demon possession is real. The question is, how can the court decide?

Faith and Facts

In here, facts are what must matter.
Ethan Thomas, lead prosecuting lawyer

'In your expert opinion . . .' is how the question is directed to the doctor specializing in psychiatry and neurology. It is revealing that the priest is never asked for his 'expert' opinion, although, presumably, he is a specialist in the area of spiritual matters. Nor is any other expert in this area called to give an opinion.

Courts of law rely on evidence that enables a judge and jury to reach a verdict that is beyond reasonable doubt. They rely on facts, evidence, exhibits and eye-witness accounts. In the case of 'The People v Father Richard Moore', the jury listen to testimony from several doctors and Father Moore himself, as well as a cassette recording of the actual exorcism. In order to make their decision, they must first decide if demons exist and if demon possession is a reality. If they do not believe in demons and demon possession, they will have to find Father Moore responsible for Emily's death. If they do believe, then they must decide if Emily was actually possessed, and if Father Moore did the right thing by trying to help her as best as he was able.

The prosecution puts forward their case that Emily suffered from a rare and extreme case of psychotic epilepsy. The specialist doctor is able to give a scientific explanation for each of her symptoms: hallucinations, violent outbursts and speaking in two voices at once. Her EEG (electro-encephalogram – a test used in the diagnosis of epilepsy) had shown possible epileptic tendencies. Her symptoms weren't typical of epilepsy, although they were typical of psychosis, which explains the diagnosis. However, the term *psychotic epilepsy* was invented by the medical expert to describe Emily's condition because he had never seen a case quite like this before.

The defence asserts that Emily Rose had been possessed by demonic powers, and that her exorcism was unsuccessful because of the medication she was taking. Through Father Moore's testimony, the recording of the exorcism, a specialist doctor testifying to the scientific credibility of demon possession, and a letter written by Emily in which she describes a visitation from the Virgin Mary explaining her demon possession, the defence puts forward a compelling case.

The problem is that the answer to the fundamental question, 'Do demons exist?' overshadows all arguments. If the jury do not believe that demons exist – however convincing the case for the defence is – they will not be able to accept it.

Belief and Reality

'Demons exist whether you believe in them or not.'
Father Moore

The jury's beliefs cannot determine whether something is actually real or not. It either is or it isn't. Demon possession could be real even if they don't believe it is. Similarly, demon possession could be believed, and yet be nothing more than a figment of the imagination of those who believe. If I believe in it, but my friend doesn't, how do we have a conversation about it? I think the film has something to teach us here.

Lead prosecutor Ethan Thomas (Campbell Scott) charges the jury with, 'Don't you *believe* it, because the *fact* is, the Devil didn't do this to Emily Rose – it was the defendant.' But defence lawyer Erin Bruner (Laura Linney) brings a slightly different perspective. She points to the prosecutor as a man of faith (he is a professing Methodist), and to herself as a woman of doubt. She says she doesn't know if she believes Father Moore's *story*, but she does believe in *him*. She says to the jury, 'This trial *isn't about facts*, it's *about possibilities* . . . is it possible?' Through speaking with Father Moore, and some strange nightly disturbances, Erin becomes more and more open to the possibility of the reality of demons.

This is where we can learn something. Let's talk to people about possibilities. Sometimes our conversations don't go very far because we're adamant about what we believe, our friends are just as strongly committed to their beliefs, and the conversation simply becomes a test of who can shout the loudest. But when we are genuinely open to discussion, when we will listen and consider other points of view, I think our friends will also think about what we have to say. Asking others to consider what could be possible, rather than what they currently believe to be true, may be more productive. But we should also be willing to do what we ask of them.

So what does the jury decide? It finds Father Moore guilty of negligent homicide. But, in a surprise move, the jury then asks to recommend a sentence to the judge. Given permission, they recommend not the ten years that this crime would normally bring, but 'time served'. They have found Father Moore guilty, but they do not want to see his punishment continued. The implication seems to be that the jury does not believe that the existence of demons is true, and therefore have to find him guilty. But they are challenged by Bruner to believe in Father Moore and to consider that it is *possible*. It is this possibility that seems to lead them to recommend a more lenient sentence. The verdict is guilty, but he leaves the court house a free man.

Our Side of the Screen

'She woke me up to things I'd never seen before.'
Jason, Emily's boyfriend

Is it the job of a court of law to make such a decision on the reality of demons? In the world of hard facts and evidence, some might say not. But if not, then whose job is it? Dealing with the spiritual realm might be considered to be the obvious job of a priest or vicar. Or maybe it's the job of the wider church or individual Christians. The question is, who will your friends be influenced by in their opinions?

Maybe the best place to start is with ourselves. We need to be thinking about what we believe to be true. Do we believe that demons exist? Do we believe that demon possession is real? Most Bible-believing Christians would find it difficult to say that they didn't believe these things. Throughout the Bible there are accounts of demon possession and subsequent exorcisms. In the gospel accounts, Jesus drives out evil spirits from possessed people (e.g. Mk. 1:23–26; 5:7–13). Some books delve more deeply into the supernatural realm. In the book of Job, the Devil enters God's presence and asks to torment Job. He believes that this will reveal that Job only worshipped God because he was blessed with riches and health, and as soon as those things are taken away, Job will give up on God (Job 1). Many Christians regard this story as a historical account implying the existence of the Devil and God.

Some Christians may also point to stories from foreign places where demon possession is reported. These stories are usually from more 'primitive' cultures in Africa or Asia. In the film, the doctor who testifies to the reality of demon possession is called 'pseudo-scientific' and a 'witch doctor' by the prosecutor, the latter term having strong associations with tribal cultures in these areas of the world. However, for Christians living in western culture, the difference between what we say we believe and the reality in which we live can be huge. We say we believe that demons exist and demon possession is real, but, deep down, we believe it only happens at other times and in other places. It happened in Bible times; it happens in Africa. Can it happen in Britain or America? Can it happen today? Well, that presents a bit more of a problem. But the film is set in small-town America and is based on a true story that took place in Germany in 1976.[2] Now that's a little closer to home.

Can we believe that demon possession could happen to us or the people around us?

Our first challenge is to decide if the Bible's picture of the supernatural realm is true for all time and in all places. Or maybe, we need to start at least by answering Erin Bruner's question, 'Is it possible?' And as we've considered already, this might be the best place to start with our friends. At the beginning of the film, Erin is utterly convinced that demons do not exist. By the end she has moved to the position of not knowing if she believes in them or not, but she thinks it might be possible. It is Father Moore's testimony that challenges her. She knows that he is utterly convinced that they are real.

Living Truth

> 'I don't care about my reputation and I'm not afraid of jail. All I care about is telling Emily Rose's story.'
>
> Father Moore

What was it about Father Moore that challenged Erin Bruner to consider the possibility of the reality of demons? He was utterly convinced of his belief and he was determined to act on it. Father Moore knew that demons were real and demon possession was a reality. He wasn't embarrassed in front of Erin because she didn't agree with him, and he showed her that he believed it. He faced the accusation of negligent homicide and a prison sentence for what he believed. Erin was totally convinced that Father Moore believed what he said because his actions matched his words. We may not get the opportunity to face a prison sentence for exorcising a demon, but the challenge to 'walk the talk' is equally there for us as Christians. In terms of the supernatural, what we believe about good and evil will influence the way we live in, and think about, our world. Is evil present in our world? Are the terrible crimes we hear about on the news the result of evil working in people? Does our own individual capacity to do wrong things stem from evil influences? What we believe about the reality of evil forces will influence the answers to these questions. And the challenge then comes as to whether we are consistent in our beliefs. We may say that we believe that demonic powers are present and active in our world. But our answers to these and other questions might betray that we don't really believe that at all.

The challenge is there for other areas of life too. Does what we say we believe match the way we live and think? We say we trust God, but we worry about having enough money, whether we're in the right job, not being able to do what we think God has called us to do and a million other things. Father Moore challenged Erin by the consistency between what he said and what he did. Do we challenge our friends by the consistency between what we say and what we do?

> I don't believe in demons but I do believe in Father Moore and I believe he believes in them. (Erin Bruner)

What if we're not too sure about what we believe? Father Moore was convinced of the reality of demons and their presence in Emily Rose; we may not be so sure. But does that mean we can't talk to others about this subject? Not necessarily. Father Moore let Erin see who he really was – what he really believed, which was proven by his actions. That's all we need to do too. We need to let our friends see who we really are –

what we really believe, which is proven by our actions. Being a Christian is about being on a journey. At the start of the journey we're not given all the answers, but our faith and our understanding grow as we experience life with God. We may not be as far down the road as Father Moore. We may believe in God, and believe the Bible teaches us about him and our world. We may know that the Bible speaks of the reality of demons and demon possession, but we may struggle to believe it ourselves. Then our friends need to see us walking our journey. We don't need to pretend that we believe something if we don't – and it will probably become obvious anyway. But we can say what we do believe. For example, we can say that we believe in God; that we believe the Bible is true; that we believe the Bible says that demons and demon possession are a reality. And then we can be honest and say that we struggle with what the Bible says, and that we are trying to work out if it is true. Having that openness not only gains credibility with people as they see our honesty, but may also make them feel more comfortable to join in a discussion.

> There are dark forces surrounding this trial ... dark powerful forces. (Father Moore)

What also influences Erin is Father Moore's concern for her. He warns her to be careful because of these dark forces. He has seen a girl he cares about tortured and killed; he's in prison, facing a charge of negligent homicide; and his lawyer has just revealed that she doesn't believe in demons – a fact on which the trial will rely. And yet, in the middle of all that, he shows genuine concern for the lawyer and wants to help her. That's a powerful message for Erin to take in. He doesn't try and win a truth battle, arguing his case and pressurizing her to agree. His actions are a natural result of his belief: he believes she is being targeted by evil forces and he warns her to be careful. And so she listens to him. Our challenge is to care for our friends in the same way.

Playing with Fire

'People say that God is dead, but how can they believe that when I show them the Devil?'
   Father Moore, quoting from a letter written by Emily

But aside from the fact that we can find something useful to learn from what we've seen, should Christians aim to avoid films like this, with such a pronounced focus on demonic powers? Scott Derrickson, the director, was asked how to avoid what some might think was a fascination with evil:

> C. S. Lewis had that very practical wisdom, well stated, in his introduction to *The Screwtape Letters*, when he talks about how the two great dangers, in regard to our thoughts about the demonic and the Devil, are to think too much of them or too little of them. To be too afraid of them, to be too hesitant to engage in discussion or thought or art that deals with this realm, is to give in to fear; but to become fascinated with it and to indulge in the material is also very unhealthy ... I really just wanted to make a film that was going to provoke the mainstream audience to ask themselves what they believe, and cause them to come away from the film provoked to think about and discuss spiritual matters and spiritual issues that I think are profoundly important.[3]

The film itself does seem to not only tell a story but to convey a belief. As the trial hinges on the question of whether demon possession is possible, so the whole atmosphere of the film seems to push this question forward. At times we see through Emily's eyes as she suffers an attack, although this could be explained as us witnessing her psychotic disorder. But then we see Father Moore experiencing very similar visual 'hallucinations', and Erin having strange nightly disturbances, both at 3.00 a.m. which is the time that Emily's attacks started. On top of this, the doctor who was present at the exorcism is suddenly killed in strange circumstances. As a viewer, you are beginning to wonder where the next demon is coming from. It seems that demon possession is very much possible.

Facing Fear

Derrickson thinks the horror genre has the potential to tackle issues of good and evil more than any other:

> To me, this genre deals more overtly with the supernatural than any other genre ... The genre is not about making you feel good, it is about making you face your fears. ... To me, the horror genre is the genre of non-denial. It's about admitting that there is evil in the world, and recognizing that there is evil within us, and that we're not in control, and that the things that we are afraid of must be confronted in order for us to relinquish that fear. And I think that the horror genre serves a great purpose in bolstering our understanding of what is evil and therefore better defining what is good.[4]

He is, however, aware that many horror films don't accomplish this:

I'm talking about, really, the potential of the horror genre, because there are a lot of horror films that don't do these things. It is a genre that's full of exploitation, but the better films in the genre certainly accomplish, I think, very noble things.[5]

It doesn't follow that we need to watch this kind of film to engage with this subject, but for Christians in the west there does seem to be some reticence to talk about the supernatural and, in particular, demonic forces. This seems to stem largely from our ignorance. Maybe films like this, or the other things from the media discussed in this book, force us to engage with these issues and help us to open up conversations with people. Scott Derrickson clearly wants to get people thinking and talking about the supernatural. And maybe we need a little nudge in the right direction to do this.

But then again, do the media give us false pictures of the supernatural, and does this undermine what we are trying to say? A review on www.christananswers. net points out:

Particularly problematic is a scene late in the film in which a possibly possessed Emily has a vision of the Virgin Mary who explains (maybe) God's purpose in allowing her to remain possessed and offering her a choice that makes more dramatic than theological sense. Derrickson, a professing Christian, understands that this scene may be problematic for some Christian viewers, stating for the record that, 'I do not believe that a spirit-filled Christian can become demon possessed.' Some Christians may look at this statement in conjunction with the film's ending and see no other plausible explanation than that Emily – as presented in the film – is not possessed. Derrickson clearly does not want viewers to read it that way, though, arguing that for 'every one' of the 'theological rules we like to systematically create there are often exceptions.'[6]

Would it be a problem to use *The Exorcism of Emily Rose* as a springboard for conversations about the supernatural if we believe that it isn't painting a completely true picture? In a way that's for each of us to answer for ourselves. But one thing we should consider is, will it create an opportunity for conversation that can then move on? I think it does. I watched the film *The Devil's Advocate* with someone who isn't a Christian and the first question they asked me on leaving the cinema was, 'Is that what you think the Devil is like?' Well, the answer was, 'Yes and no.' And the opportunity was there to move the conversation on and talk about it.

Ultimately, as Christians, we need to share our faith with our friends. Sometimes this seems too difficult. But if we can create opportunities and begin to take them, we may find it's possible. *The Exorcism of Emily Rose* teaches us to work out what we think is true; to make sure our actions match what we say; to be honest about where we are on our journey to discovering the truth; and to show people that we care about them. In a world where the supernatural seems to be of increasing interest – out of the six trailers before this film, four were directly associated with supernatural evil – this is one area where we need to be searching out the truth, thinking through what we believe and trying to talk to our friends about it.

Notes

[1] Peter T. Chattaway, 'Horror: The Perfect Christian Genre', *Christianity Today*, 30 August 2005 – www.christianitytoday.com/movies/interviews/scottderrickson.html

[2] A twenty-three-year-old German woman called Anneliese Michel died from malnutrition and dehydration after a year of twice-weekly exorcisms, during which time she hardly ate. Her story was written up by the anthropologist Dr Felicitas Goodman in her book, *How about Demons?: Possession and Exorcism in the Modern World* (Indiana University Press, 1988)

[3] Chattaway, 'Horror: The Perfect Christian Genre'

[4] Chattaway, 'Horror: The Perfect Christian Genre'

[5] Chattaway, 'Horror: The Perfect Christian Genre'

[6] Kenneth R. Moreland, 'Movie Review: *The Exorcism of Emily Rose*', *Christian Spotlight on the Movies*, – www.christiananswers.net/spotlight/movies/2005/theexorcismofemilyrose2005.html

Hell is waking up every Goddamn day
and not even knowing why you're here.

Marv in the film *Sin City*

7. *Lost* – Study Guide

Emily Dalrymple

TV Series Title: Lost
Writers: J.J. Abrams, Damon Lindelof, David Fury, Christian Taylor, Javier Grillo-Marxuach, Jennifer Johnson and others
Directors: J.J. Abrams, Jack Bender, Kevin Hooks, Greg Yaitanes, Tucker Gates and others
Starring: Matthew Fox, Evangeline Lily, Josh Holloway, Terry O'Quinn, Dominic Monaghan, Naveen Andrews, Emilie De Ravin, Jorge Garcia, Maggie Grace, Ian Somerhalder, Daniel Dae Kim, Yunjin Kim
Production Company: Touchstone
Broadcaster: ABC (USA); Channel 4 (UK)
First Broadcast: 22 September 2004 (USA); 3 August 2005 (UK)

Key Themes

Life, death, communities, values, fear, change, choice, isolation

Summary of Season One

When a plane, which is a thousand miles off course, crashes on a remote Pacific island, only forty-eight of the passengers survive. While some panic, others discover reserves of inner strength. They scavenge whatever they can from the wrecked plane, but soon water is low. When Jack (Matthew Fox), a neurosurgeon and natural leader, finds some caves with plenty of fresh water as well as shelter, half of the survivors move into them, while the other half insists on staying at the beach in order to be visible to any rescue party. When the food runs out, the mysterious Locke (Terry O'Quinn) shows astonishing outback skills and begins teaching others how to catch boar.

All the survivors seem to have strange pasts, which are revealed in flashback in each episode. Michael (Harold Perrineau Jr) hardly knows his son Walt (Malcolm David Kelley) due to his separation from the boy's mother. But after her sudden death, her second husband claimed that there was something different about Walt and begged Michael to take him. On the island, Walt is more interested in getting to know Locke than his father. Locke also believes there is something odd about Walt who has incredible luck and experiences premonitions.

There are surprises lurking in the jungle, including a roaring, unseen monster. Former Iraqi Republican Guard Sayid (Naveen Andrews) is kidnapped by a crazed French woman named Danielle (Mira Furlan) who has been on the island for over sixteen years. He discovers that she shot the other members of her scientific expedition, including her lover, believing they were sick. He also discovers that her child was taken from her.

A new island menace emerges when one of the survivors, Ethan (William Mapother), is shockingly revealed not to be a survivor of the crash, but someone else who was already on the island. He kidnaps heavily pregnant Claire (Emilie de Ravin) and junkie rock musician Charlie (Dominic Monaghan). Jack and Kate, deep in the jungle on the trail of their missing friends, find Charlie blindfolded and hanging limply from a tree. They revive him, but he can remember nothing. Later, Claire is found wandering in the jungle, also having lost her memory of everything since boarding the plane. Ethan begins killing the survivors, making it clear he wants Claire back. When the survivors manage to trap him, Charlie kills him.

Locke finds a concealed hatch in the island floor, but keeps it secret until Danielle comes to the camp, saying that the 'Others' are coming. Locke suggests the hatch as a good place to hide. When the survivors open it, they find themselves looking down a long shaft into darkness.

Meanwhile, some of the survivors have built a raft to escape the island. Michael, Jin (Daniel Dae Kim), Walt and Sawyer (Josh Holloway) sail off on it, but deep into the night, a boat finds them. Its occupants shoot Sawyer, blow up the raft and take Walt.

Background

Lost was already a big hit in the USA by the time it started causing a stir in the UK. The second season began in the USA in September 2005, while series one was still in its early stages in the UK. It has been a huge success with television critics as well as with audiences, and won six out of the twelve Emmy awards for which it was nominated in 2005. *Lost* was created by J.J. Abrams (writer of *Armageddon* and creator of *Alias)* and Damon Lindelof. It is filmed entirely on location in Hawaii and takes its inspiration from the reality TV show *Survivor*, as well as William Golding's *Lord of the Flies.*

While acknowledging the lack of reality in the survival of so many people (and their luggage, complete with several changes of clothes), Mark Lawson says that 'the series has a commendable feel for the psychological reality of contemporary life' with the changed relation-ship between Americans and aeroplanes since 9/11.[1] Writing in *The Times*, Benji Wilson comments that, 'almost every scene contains some kind of plot twist or cliffhanger. It's this succession of whos, whats and whys that makes it so addictive'.[2] He says the weekly trick is to have 'a plot twist so fantastical that it lurches towards being absurd, and then, through a mix of taut scripting and a carefully cultivated sense of the surreal, make it believable. This kind of U-turn takes place, on average, at least three times an episode.'

Questions for Discussion

1. What do you think are the strengths of *Lost*? Are you surprised by how popular it is? Why/why not? Is there anything you don't like about it? How effective do you find the flashbacks for a particular character in each episode?

2. How would you feel and respond if you were one of the survivors of Flight 815? Which group would you stay with: the group which moved inland to find a safer place, or the group which stayed on the beach to be seen by rescuers? Why?

3. Which characters do you think would be your friends if you were on the island? Why? Who don't you like? How has your opinion of the characters changed over the course of the series? Why?

4. Mark Lawson writes in *The Guardian:*

   > *Lost* . . . is a fantasy in which Americans (and, by extension, America) survive a terrible aeroplane incident but the society that results is more savage, suspicious and selfish than what existed before.[3]

   To what extent do you agree with this comment? How are savagery, suspicion and selfishness seen in the series? Do you think the behaviour of the characters is exaggerated simply to make good drama, or do you think it is a good reflection of how life might be in such extreme circumstances?

5. What motivates Sawyer? In what ways has he become a more sympathetic character as the series progresses? Do you understand him better after episode 8, 'Confidence Man'?

6. What representations of love does *Lost* offer? Which of the budding relationships featured in the show (Jack and Kate, Kate and Sawyer, Claire and Charlie, Shannon and Sayid) do you think will last? How do they compare to Jin and Sun's broken marriage?

7. How well do you think Kate handles the rivalry between Jack and Sawyer? How does knowing that Kate killed someone change your opinion of her? How does it change the survivors' opinions of her? Is Sawyer right when he claims that neither

he nor Kate belong (episode 16, 'Outlaws')? Why/ Why not?

8. 'If we can't live together, we're going to die alone.' (Jack, episode 5, 'White Rabbit')

   What values does the community of survivors need to have in order to function as a community? Where do you think values come from – are they a means of enabling the species to survive, are they part of how God made us, or do we learn them from God's revelation (see, for example, Ps. 119:1– 16; Mic. 6:6–8; Rom. 2:12–16)?

9. 'Well, we all have our temptations. But giving in to them, that's your choice. As we live our lives, it's really nothing but a series of choices.' (Priest, episode 7, 'The Moth')

   'If I [disposed of the drugs] you wouldn't have a choice, Charlie. And having choices, making decisions based on more than instinct is the only thing that separates you from [the boar].' (Locke, episode 7, 'The Moth')

   How have Charlie's previous choices brought him to this point in his life? What is the significance of the moth? After making this choice, why do you think he makes a different choice in one of the final episodes (episode 24, 'Exodus Part 2')? What is the programme suggesting about whether humans are governed by their upbringing and environment or by their own free choices (see, for example, Prov. 22:6; Rom. 1:18–32)?

10. How do the survivors handle their fear of the unknown?

11. Do you think that Hurley is cursed? Why/why not? Do you believe in curses? How does this fit with the biblical perspective of suffering (see, for example, Hab. 3:16–18; Lk. 13:1–5; Rom. 8:18–39)?

12. How does Boone's death affect the survivors? Who is the most changed by the event? Why? Why did the programme makers show Boone's death alongside Claire giving birth? How did it make you feel? Why?

13. How else does *Lost* deal with the subject of death? What does our view of death reveal about our understanding of the nature of human beings? Compare the views of death in *Lost* with those found in the Bible (see, for example, Job 19:25–27; Ecc. 9:1–10; 1 Cor. 15:50–57; 2 Cor. 5:1–10).

14. 'I want to tell you that you're special, very special. You're part of a design, you do realise that don't you?' (Locke's mother Emily, episode 19, 'Deus Ex Machina')

    'No one's punishing us. There's no such thing as fate.' (Claire, episode 25, 'Exodus Part 2')

    What attitudes towards fate or providence are seen in *Lost*? How does this fit with a Christian understanding of God and his sovereignty (see, for example, Gen. 50:15–21; Is. 46:3–13; Gal. 6:7–9)?

15. What does the building of the raft represent to the survivors?

16. How do you think Ethan Rom got onto the island? How has his presence changed the survivors? Is Charlie right when he claims Ethan deserved to

die (episode 15, 'Homecoming')? Have any of us got the right to make judgements like that (see Gen. 9:5–6; Rom. 12:17–21, for example)? How does Charlie's attitude compare with the New Testament concept of grace?

17. Why do you think the 'others' want Walt? How is his kidnapping likely to affect the survivors? How might it affect his father Michael?

Notes

[1] Mark Lawson, 'After the crash . . .', *The Guardian*, 5 August 2005 – media.guardian.co.uk/site/story/0,14173,1542935,00.html

[2] Benji Wilson, 'Board the flight to the Lost world', *The Times*, 6 August 2005 – entertainment.timesonline.co.uk/article/0,,14934-1717694,00.html

[3] Lawson, 'After the crash . . .'

It doesn't always make sense, and most of it never happened. But that's the kind of story this is.

Ed Bloom in the film *Big Fish*

8. *Jonathan Strange and Mr Norrell* – Study Guide

Louise Crook

Book Title: Jonathan Strange and Mr Norrell
Author: Susanna Clarke
Publisher: Bloomsbury
Publication Date: 30 September 2004

Key Themes

Magic, fantasy, friendship, rivalry, jealousy, love, class, society

Summary

Jonathan Strange and Mr Norrell charts an alternative version of nineteenth-century England where magic underpins the whole society. Mr Norrell of Hurtfew Abbey is a recluse who has a secret: he is a 'practical' magician. He is angered by the re-forming in 1806 of the Learned Society of York Magicians, as the group are only theoretical magicians. These theoretical magicians have no ability to practise magic, but instead spend endless hours debating England's magical past and future. This re-forming of the Learned Society of York Magicians spurs Mr Norrell into action, and he causes the statues in York Cathedral to talk – and to tell their long-hidden secrets. This act persuades many that magic has returned to England, and excitement begins to grow around the country. Mr Norrell, who is not particularly fond of human company, is persuaded by his servant Childermass to move to London and promote himself in fashionable society in order to revolutionise the English magic scene that he so hates. His aim is not to revive magic for the masses, however. He wants to keep tight control of its practice by restricting access to his books and by propounding his own ideas; Mr Norrell is a proud and jealous man.

Jonathan Strange is the son of a cruel but rich man from whom he inherits a large fortune. He is married to his beloved Arabella, a lively woman who is devoted to her husband. A series of coincidental events leads Strange to a small village where he meets Vinculus, a ragged street magician. Vinculus delivers a prophecy to him about the future of English magic and the role Strange will play in it. Strange purchases a few spells from Vinculus, and so begins his magical career. He knows of Mr Norrell's growing notoriety and decides to seek him out so that he can receive more formal training.

Mr Norrell is initially suspicious, but soon comes to delight in the idea of having a pupil, while Jonathan Strange learns to deal with Norrell's eccentricities. However, this enthusiasm does not last long. Strange becomes increasingly interested in John Uskglass, the Raven King who once ruled both human and faerie kingdoms. At the same time, his desire to be controlled by Mr Norrell dwindles and their relationship deteriorates.

The revival of English magic, in which Jonathan Strange and Mr Norrell play such a significant role, has far-reaching consequences for themselves, their friends and, indeed, the whole world – especially when the revival takes a more sinister turn than either of them ever intended.

Background

Susanna Clarke's *Jonathan Strange and Mr Norrell* has taken the literary world by storm since its publication in hardback in September 2004. It is an epic part-fantasy, part-historical tale of over a thousand pages, and has been sold in over thirty countries. The book deliberately echoes the style of both Jane Austen and George Elliot, as well as being clearly influenced by J.R.R. Tolkien. It has inevitably been compared to J.K. Rowling's *Harry Potter* novels because they both have magic as their subject matter. But in fact *Jonathan Strange and Mr Norrell* is a very different sort of novel.

Susanna Clarke took twelve years to write *Jonathan Strange and Mr Norrell*, which is not surprising when you consider its length and the scrupulous historical research which must have gone into it. Clarke was born in 1959 and is the daughter of a Methodist minister. She studied at Oxford University before going into publishing and working for a short while in Spain and Italy. *Jonathan Strange and Mr Norrell* is her first novel, and was written while Clarke was working as editor of a cookery list.

Jonathan Strange and Mr Norrell has received rave reviews on both sides of the Atlantic. It was on the long list for the Man Booker Prize 2004 and was short-listed for both the *Guardian* First Book Award and the

Whitbread First Novel Award. A *Sunday Times* review praises the book because it is:

> ... in both the precise and the colloquial sense, a fabulous book ... the subject matter of Susanna Clarke's first novel is – much of it – beyond belief, and the author's achievement in writing it is almost as prodigious ... This is a novel large enough to provide an immense range of pleasures.[1]

A film version of the novel is already in the pipeline (to be made by New Line Cinema who brought us *Lord of the Rings)*, and Susanna Clarke has an army of devoted fans who eagerly await her next offering.

Questions for Discussion

1. What did you think of *Jonathan Strange and Mr Norrell?* Why?

2. How are the main themes of the novel developed as the story progresses?

3. How would you describe the style of the novel? What effect does this style have on the story?

4. How convincing do you think Susanna Clarke's portrayal of an 'alternative' history of Britain is? What kind of portrait does it paint of Regency England?

5. How do you react to Mr Norrell? In what ways do you think he is a changed man by the end of the story?

6. What do you think of Jonathan Strange? How would you describe him? What is it that motivates his search for the Raven King?

7. How does Strange's love for Arabella shape his life? What role does marriage play in *Jonathan Strange and Mr Norrell*?

8. To what extent are Strange and Norrell motivated by different things in reviving magic in Britain? What do you think of their respective motivations? How do their personalities differ, and how are they similar?

9. How are those in authority portrayed in the novel? What are we encouraged to make of the government ministers, aristocrats and those in charge of the army?

10. What does this novel have to say about class, and, in particular, the difference between those who are 'gentlemen' and those who are not?

11. Why do you think magic was so fascinating to our ancestors, and still has such a grip on the imagination in our society today? What does this say about our human longings and human nature?

12. What role does Vinculus' prophecy play in *Jonathan Strange and Mr Norrell*? How does this relate to the role prophecy plays in the Bible (see, for example, Is. 7:1–9; Is. 53; Hos. 4:1–7; 1 Pet. 1:20–21)?

13. What role does the 'gentleman with the thistle-down hair' play in *Jonathan Strange and Mr Norrell*? What do you think he represents?

14. How is the dark side of magic presented in the novel? Does magic become a force for good or evil? Why? To what extent do you think this could be interpreted as a representation of the spiritual battle for good and evil in our world (see Eph. 6:10–18)?

15. How do Strange and Norrell come to realise their own smallness in the magical world? How does this relate to our smallness before God (see Ps. 8:3–4; Is. 40:12–31)?

16. Why do you think Susanna Clarke uses so much biblical imagery in *Jonathan Strange and Mr Norrell*? What is your opinion of the way in which she uses this imagery?

17. Susanna Clarke has commented that:

> It never really occurred to me that there would be a problem with magic and Christianity co-existing. After all, for much of our history magic and Christianity did co-exist, in the sense that there were people who believed in both. . . . Obviously in Strange and Norrell's world, magic has been part of the established order for a long time, so magicians and churchmen have had to find a way to accommodate each other. I don't exactly see them in opposition to each other – magicians and clergymen are both dealing with what's beyond this world. Strange and Norrell would both have considered themselves Christians, like the vast majority of the population in those days.[2]

Are Christianity and magic compatible, as Clarke suggests, or are they opposed to each other? To what extent can you believe in both Christianity and magic? How do you react to Clarke's comment that Strange and Norrell would regard themselves as Christians? What does Romans 10:9–10 suggest it means to be a Christian (see also Jn. 3:16–21; 1 Jn. 5:1–5)?

18. John Uskglass has large numbers of dedicated followers who wait for him and put their hope and trust in him. Why do you think this is? What

hope does he offer? How does this compare to Jesus' earthly ministry? What hope does Jesus Christ offer us (see Jn. 3:16, 36; 5:24; 8:36; Rom. 6:23; 1 Pet. 1:3–6)? What different things do people in our society today put their hope and trust in, and how does that compare to the hope the Bible shows us is available through Jesus?

19. What is Lost-hope? How does the idea that there is more to reality than we can see in this world manifest itself in *Jonathan Strange and Mr Norrell*? What evidence does the Bible offer us about life after death (see Mt. 28:5–10; 1 Cor. 15:12–20), and what difference might this make to the way in which we talk to our friends?

20. What role does death play in *Jonathan Strange and Mr Norrell*? How is the idea of resurrection used in the novel? What does the Bible teach about death and resurrection (see Heb. 9:27; Ecc. 3:18–21; 1 Cor. 15:3–5, 21–28, 42–56)? How could you use Susanna Clarke's portrayal of death and resurrection in *Jonathan Strange and Mr Norrell* to talk to a non-Christian friend about the gospel?

Notes

[1] www.JonathanStrange.com

[2] Liz Williams and Claire Weaver, 'Getting Familiar with Strange: A chat with Susanna Clarke', *Broad Universe*, 25 May 2005 – www.broaduniverse.org

I think to believe in life after death you would have to believe in God, and if I believed in God I would have to forgo a lot of my other rational and scientific beliefs. It would mean a complete restructuring of the way I see the world.

Simon Armitage

9. Chasing After the Wind –
Logical Positivism and A.J. Ayer

Peter S. Williams

There was a time, not so very long ago in the early twentieth century, when thinking about God was an activity nearly banished from academia because many people thought that talk about 'God' was *literally meaningless*. They thought talking about 'God' made as much literal sense as the sort of cooing noises adults habitually make to babies: 'Coochie Coochie Coo!' In other words, they thought that 'God-talk' made no sense at all (beyond its emotive content). God was not the only subject to suffer such banishment. Assertions about right and wrong, beauty and ugliness – indeed, all statements that were metaphysical in nature – were widely considered to be literally *nonsense*.

The enforcer of this philosophical dress code, the bouncer on the door of academically respectable conversation topics, was the now infamous 'verification principle' put forward by a group of thinkers collectively known as 'logical positivists'. Philosopher Kelly James Clark explains that logical positivism, 'began in the early 1920s in an informal discussion group in Austria called the Vienna Circle. The original members, led by physicist Moritz Schlick, included mathematicians, physicists, sociologists and economists but no professional philosophers.'[1] This omission was unfortunate, because, 'United by their passionate dislike of the metaphysical – the realm beyond the . . . physical world – the group developed a unified philosophy that embraced science and attempted to destroy philosophy.'[2]

Attempting to develop a unified philosophy that dispenses with philosophy makes about as much sense as Groucho Marx's comment that he wouldn't belong to any club that would have him as a member. Nevertheless, the ideas of the Vienna Circle spread far and wide. The ghost of their attitude towards metaphysics in general – and God in particular – continues to haunt parts of western academia to this day.

Despite some disagreement among the members of the Vienna Circle, 'there was an initial impulse to accept the verification theory of meaning . . .'[3] This theory held that any statement that was not true by definition (e.g. 'all bachelors are unmarried men') was only meaningful if it could be empirically verified – at least in principle. To 'empirically verify' something means to check it out with the physical senses (sight, hearing, touch, etc). In other words, the statement, 'This is a book', *is meaningful* because you can verify it by seeing, touching and even smelling this book. But a statement like, 'The sunset is beautiful', *is not meaningful* because you cannot verify its meaning by seeing or touching or smelling beauty. You can see *the sunset*, but you can't see an additional objective reality called *beauty* over and above the physical phenomenon of the sunset. Likewise, the statement, 'God exists', is not meaningful because you cannot verify that either. You can't literally see, touch or taste God. According to logical positivism, 'God exists' is therefore not a meaningful statement that is either true or false, but a use of language on a par with nonsense poetry (like the parts of 'Jabberwocky' that Lewis Caroll didn't define). It may have an emotional resonance, but it has no rational content that can be understood or judged as being either an accurate representation or an inaccurate representation of reality.

Positivism by Ayer Mail

The primary importer of logical positivism to Britain was A.J. Ayer (1910–1989). Unlike the members of the Vienna Circle, Alfred Jules Ayer (known to his friends as 'Freddie') was a philosopher. Educated in the humanities at Eton College, Ayer studied philosophy at Oxford under Gilbert Ryle before becoming a professor himself, ending up back at Oxford (1947–1959) for a time. Ayer served in the British military during World War Two, including a stint in Military Intelligence.

Ayer was immersed in logical positivism during 1932 whilst studying (at Ryle's recommendation) with Moritz Schlick in Vienna. This visit filled the gap between Ayer's university finals and taking up his first lectureship. Two years later, Ayer started work on the book that would make his name: a presentation of logical positivism called *Language, Truth and Logic*, which was published in 1936:

> Ayer's philosophical ideas were largely parasitic on those of the Vienna Circle. However, his clear, vibrant and (arguably) arrogant exposition of them makes *Language, Truth and Logic* essential reading on the tenets of logical positivism – the book is a classic, and is widely read in philosophy courses around the world.[4]

Following the Vienna Circle, Ayer proclaimed:

The term 'God' is a metaphysical term. And if 'God' is a metaphysical term, then it cannot even be probable that a god exists. For to say that 'God exists' is to make a metaphysical utterance which cannot be either true or false ... If a putative proposition fails to satisfy [the verification] principle, and is not a tautology, then ... it is metaphysical, and ... being metaphysical, it is neither true nor false but literally senseless.[5]

As Ayer admitted, positivism entailed that the denial of God's existence was just as meaningless as the affirmation of his existence; atheism as irrational as theism: 'If the assertion that there is a god is nonsensical, then the atheist's assertion that there is no god is equally nonsensical.'[6] Not only does Ayer's verification principle exclude all objective talk about God (whether theistic *or* atheistic) from the realm of meaningful utterances, but all talk of objective goodness and beauty as well. According to Ayer:

Such aesthetic words as 'beautiful' and 'hideous' are employed, not to make statements of fact, but simply to express certain feelings and evoke a certain response. It follows, as in ethics, that there is no sense in attributing objective validity to aesthetic judgements, and no possibility of arguing about questions of value in aesthetics ... there is nothing in aesthetics, any more than there is in ethics, to justify the view that it embodies a unique type of knowledge. It should now be clear that the only information which we can legitimately derive from the study of our aesthetic and moral experiences is information about our own mental and physical make-up.[7]

Ayer's contemporary, Catholic philosopher F.C. Copleston, observed that: 'Ayer's writings [have] exercised a widespread influence, particularly perhaps on university students, for whom it possessed the charm of novelty and an atmosphere of daring.'[8] Playwright William Cash calls Ayer, 'arguably the most influential twentieth century rationalist after Bertrand Russell'.[9] Ayer's declaration that God-talk was nonsense influenced an entire generation of scholars, despite *Language, Truth and Logic* only selling in small numbers initially. Hilary Spurling observes that, when it was published, it sold

> . . . just over 1,000 copies (64 years later, the book still sells 2,000 a year in Britain: a 1945 reprint in the United States has sold 300,000). It was one of those books that galvanise a whole generation. Ambitious undergraduates commonly read it at a sitting. Their elders were appalled. When students tried to discuss the book at an Oxford seminar, the Master of Balliol flung it through the window. Ayer was denounced by a housemaster at Winchester School as the wickedest man in Oxford. Asked what came next, the young iconoclast said cheerfully: 'There's no next. Philosophy has come to an end. Finished.'[10]

A Negative Assessment of Logical Positivism

In 1943, E.L. Mascall observed that, 'the logical positivists' position seems to be crumbling from within.'[11] Just two decades after *Language, Truth and Logic* was published, F.C. Copleston could write, 'there are few British philosophers who willingly accept the title of 'positivists' or who make open profession of applying the principle of verifiability as a criterion of meaning . . . [positivism] is no longer fashionable.'[12] A number of factors explain the demise of positivism.

Verifying God

As philosopher John Hick pointed out, when made precise enough, the statement that 'God exists' *is* empirically verifiable (at least *in principle*, which is all that the principle of verification requires). Hick argued that:

> A set of expectations based upon faith in the historic Jesus as the incarnation of God, and in his teaching as being divinely authoritative, could be so fully confirmed in *post-mortem* experience as to leave no grounds for rational doubt as to the validity of that faith.[13]

If you were to die and then find yourself in a clearly *Christian* afterlife – that is, you are given a resurrected body and a life in a community of Christians that revolves around the resurrected and ascended Jesus Christ – one could surely count this experience as an *indirect* empirical verification of God's existence. Just as empirical measurement of the background radiation of the universe provides *indirect* empirical verification of the Big Bang in cosmology (to see one isn't to see the other, but to see the one is to see something from which the other can be inferred),[14] so experiencing the sort of afterlife promised in the New Testament would likewise provide indirect empirical verification of God's existence. This being so, the claim that God exists *is* open to verification *in principle*, and therefore counts as being a meaningful claim according to the principle of verification. As Hick concluded, 'the existence or non-existence of the God of the New Testament is a matter of fact, and claims as such eventual experiential verification.'[15]

Unless positivism is framed broadly enough to allow this sort of *indirect* verification, many explanatory entities within science would count as nonsense, because they are verified indirectly (being inferred from observation of their hypothesised effects). For example, scientific theories about so-called 'dark matter' would count as meaningless under the verification principle if it excluded indirect verification.[16] The verification principle cannot be used to wall off scientific claims about the universe from religious claims about its creator, because however it is formulated, it either lets too much or too little into the category of 'claims that are meaningful'. Hence, as philosopher Lloyd Eby observes: 'All attempts to solve this problem of having a version of the verification principle ... that admits all scientific statements but excludes all metaphysical statements have met with failure.'[17]

It might be argued that the God hypothesis is not only verifiable *in principle* (as Hick argued) but also *in practice*, since several of the arguments for God can be framed using the scientific method of indirect verification (e.g. arguments for design, arguments from miracles, personal transformation, etc).[18] As Basil Mitchell comments:

> ... the Logical Positivist movement started as an attempt to make a clear demarcation between science and common sense on the one hand, and metaphysics and theology on the other. But work in the philosophy of science convinced people that what the Logical Postitivists had said about science was not true, and, by the time the philosophers of science had developed and amplified their accounts of how rationality works in science, people discovered that similar accounts applied equally well to the areas which they had previously sought to exclude, namely theology and metaphysics.[19]

Ironically for those materialists who embraced logical positivism, 'materialism would have to be rejected as nonsense by a strict interpretation of logical positivism.'[20] The claim that matter is objectively real is, after all, neither true by definition nor something that can be verified by sense data (since it is the nature of what the senses perceive that is in question). Positivism makes not only materialism, but also a realist account of science, impossible. As F.C. Copleston argued in his famous BBC debate on positivism with Ayer:

> ... if the meaning of an existential proposition consists, according to the principle, in its verifiability, it is impossible, I think, to escape an infinite regress, since the verification will still itself need verification, and so on indefinitely. If this is so, then all [existential] propositions, including scientific ones, are meaningless.[21]

Verificationism is either self-contradictory or arbitrary

Finally, as R. Douglas Geivett explains, chief among the woes of logical positivism was the fact that the verification principle 'was neither empirically verifiable nor tautological'.[22] That is, the verification principle was *itself* a metaphysical claim – a claim that therefore ruled itself to be meaningless. '*It failed its own requirement* for factual meaningfulness,' notes William P. Alston, 'and thus was self-refuting.'[23] Roger Scruton observes: 'Logical positivism no longer has a following, and it is easy to see why. The verification principle cannot be verified: it therefore condemns itself as meaningless.'[24] As Copleston argued in his debate with Ayer:

> ... the principle of verification ... is either a proposition or no proposition. If it is, it must be, on your premises, either a tautology or an empirical hypothesis. If the

former, no conclusion follows as to metaphysics. If the latter, the principle itself would require verification. But the principle of verification cannot itself be verified. If, however, the principle is not a proposition, it must, on your premises, be meaningless.[25]

Ayer tried to get around this problem by admitting that the verification principle wasn't a meaningful *proposition* but saying that it was a *rule* for using language. But why pay attention to such an arbitrary rule? As Ayer himself asked, 'Why should anyone follow the prescription if its implications were not to his taste?'[26] Philosopher Keith Ward reports the following conversation between Ayer and a student:

> A student once asked [Ayer] if you could make any true general statement about meaningful statements. 'Yes,' he replied. 'You can say that all meaningful statements must be verifiable in principle.' 'I see what you mean,' said the student. 'But how can I verify that?' 'I am glad you asked that,' said the philosopher. 'You cannot verify it. But it is not really a meaningful statement; it is just a rule for using language.' 'Whose rule?' 'Well, it's my rule, really. But it is a very useful one. If you use it, you will find you agree with me completely. I think that would be very useful.'[27]

If we adopted the rule, then of course we would agree with Ayer, and of course Ayer would find that useful! But he cannot provide us with a *reason* for adopting his rule – certainly not one that doesn't implicitly contradict the rule he wants us to adopt. Instead, he recommends it on the basis of its usefulness. Useful for what? For insulating a worldview that excludes everything metaphysical – especially religion (as shown by the positivists' failed attempts to produce a version of the principle capable of drawing a line of demarcation between science on the one hand, and religion on the other). Indeed, at heart I suspect that the motivation behind logical positivism is the desire to exclude God by excluding talk about God. Logical positivism was quite simply a form of atheistic censorship. However, the younger generation of philosophers, like Ward, who opposed this baseless peer-pressure were well within their rights to point out that the emperor of positivism had no clothes, but brazenly walked the halls of academia with nothing but a smile of fashionable popularity to disguise his self-contradicting ways.

The Verdict on Verificationism

James Kelly Clark describes the verification principle as a piece of, 'unjustifiable philosophical imperialism that, in the end, could not survive critical scrutiny'.[28] William Lane Craig comments: 'Fifty years ago philosophers widely regarded talk about God as literally meaningless . . . but today no informed philosopher could take such a viewpoint.'[29] Ronald H. Nash concludes that logical positivism 'is dead and quite properly so'.[30] Ayer himself mused: 'I just stated [the verification rule] dogmatically and an extraordinary number of people seemed to be convinced by my assertion.'[31] By 1973, Ayer admitted that, 'the verification principle is defective'.[32] Talking about positivism during an interview in 1978, Ayer conceded: 'Nearly all of it was false.'[33] Philosopher Roy Abraham Varghese reports Ayer as affirming: 'Logical positivism died a long time ago. I don't think much of *Language, Truth and Logic* is true. I think it is full of mistakes.'[34]

Rationalist Prize Fighter

Despite admitting that logical positivism was flawed, Ayer continued not to believe in God:

> Ayer was closely associated with the British humanist movement. He was an Honorary Associate of the Rationalist Press Association from 1947 until his death. In 1965, he became the first president of the Agnostics' Adoption Society and in the same year succeeded Julian Huxley as president of the British Humanist Association, a post he held until 1970.[35]

In the late 1940s, Ayer was 'employed by the BBC to take on such opponents as Hugh Montefiore, Bishop of Birmingham, and Jesuit priest Martin D'Arcy, a friend of Evelyn Waugh, and to broadcast his vigorously humanist views.'[36] In the 1950s, Ayer's audience could see him as a guest on the TV panel discussion programme *The Brains Trust*.[37] Ayer taught or lectured several times in the United States. In 1987 he served as a visiting professor at Bard College:

> At a party that same year held by fashion designer Fernando Sanchez, Ayer, then 77, confronted Mike Tyson harassing Naomi Campbell. When Ayer demanded that Tyson stop, the boxer said: 'Do you know who the ... I am? I'm the heavyweight champion of the world,' to which Ayer replied: 'And I am the former Wykeham Professor of Logic. We are both pre-eminent in our field. I suggest that we talk about this like rational men.'[38]

From Ayer to Eternity

In June of 1988, Ayer clinically 'died' in London University Hospital: his heart stopping for four minutes after he choked on some food. Ayer was discharged in early July and re-married his second wife, Dee Wells. He also published two articles recounting a near-death experience in which he was pulled toward an 'exceedingly bright, and also very painful' red light, encountered the 'ministers' of the universe and was frustrated by trying to 'cross the river' (which he presumed was the River Styx of Greek mythology). However, he also publicly re-affirmed his lack of belief in an afterlife. This episode continues to generate controversy, with the recent suggestion that there are discrepancies between Ayer's public and private comments about his near-death experience raising the question of whether Ayer in fact genuinely believed that he had met God during those four minutes.

Whilst writing a play for the Edinburgh Festival about Ayer's near-death experience, William Cash received a letter from Dr Jeremy George, the senior registrar in charge of Ayer while he was hospitalised (and a student at New College Oxford in the 1970s, when Ayer was the Wykeham Professor of Logic). George recounted how:

> I asked [Ayer], as a philosopher, what was it like to have had a near-death experience? He suddenly looked rather sheepish. Then he said, 'I saw a Divine Being. I'm afraid I'm going to have to revise all my various books and opinions.' He clearly said 'Divine Being' . . . He was confiding in me, and I think he was slightly embarrassed because it was unsettling for him as an atheist. He spoke in a very confidential manner. I think he felt he had come face to face with God, or his maker, or what one might say was God. Later, when I read his article, I was surprised to

see he had left out all mention of it. I was simply amused. I wasn't very familiar with his philosophy at the time of the incident, so the significance wasn't immediately obvious. I didn't realise he was a logical positivist.[39]

Cash wrote an article about his research into Ayer's experience, reporting the comments of Ayer's son, Nick:

All this stuff about crossing the River Styx – it just sounds too good to be true. There was three months between his time in hospital and when he decided to write the article in France. He never mentioned any of that business once. And I was with him all the time. I always thought it sounded more like a dream.[40]

Cash raises the following question:

. . . can Ayer's memory or his own words really be trusted? Freddie always claimed he devoted his life to the pursuit of Truth. But as Dee Wells was quick to point out when I visited her . . . the truth could rapidly become meaningless for Freddie when it happened to suit him – with women, for example. Certainly it does seem very odd that Ayer . . . did not so much as mention his conversation with Dr George about having to rewrite all his books and works . . .[41]

The near-death experience certainly seems to have changed Ayer for the better: 'Freddie became so much nicer after he died,' said Dee. 'He was not nearly so boastful. He took an interest in other people.'[42] Ironically for a man who had propounded a philosophical principal that labelled talk about beauty as literally meaningless, Ayer reportedly told writer Edward St. Aubyn:

... that he had had 'a kind of resurrection' and for the first time in his life, he had begun to notice scenery. In France, on a mountain near his villa, he said, 'I suddenly stopped and looked out at the sea and thought, my God, how beautiful this is ... for 26 years I had never really looked at it before.'[43]

It is certainly interesting to observe that:

at the end of his life, Freddie spent more and more time with his former BBC debating opponent, the Jesuit priest and philosopher Frederick Copleston, who was at Freddie's funeral at Golders Green crematorium. 'They got closer and closer and, in the end, he was Freddie's closest friend,' said Dee. 'It was quite extraordinary ...'[44]

The Resurrection of God-Talk

On 8 April 1966, *Time Magazine* ran a cover story about the then current 'death-of-God' movement in American theology entitled 'Is God Dead?' William Lane Craig explains that:

According to the movement's protagonists, traditional theism was no longer tenable and had to be once and for all abandoned. Ironically, however, at the same time that theologians were writing God's obituary, a new generation of young philosophers was rediscovering His vitality.[45]

Only a few years later, *Time* carried a cover story asking, 'Is God coming back to life?' Interest in the philosophy of religion continued to grow to the point where, in 1980, *Time* found itself running a story about 'Modernizing the case for God', describing the contemporary movement among philosophers putting new life into the arguments for God's existence:

In a quiet revolution in thought and argument that hardly anybody could have foreseen only two decades ago, God is making a comeback. Most intriguingly, this is happening not amongst theologians or ordinary believers, but in the crisp intellectual circles of academic philosophers, where the consensus had long banished the Almighty from fruitful discourse.[46]

The reference to 'banishing the Almighty from fruitful discourse' is a reference to logical positivism. Hence, it is no surprise to find Tyler Burge, Professor of Philosophy at UCLA, writing that the central event in philosophy during the last half century was, 'the downfall of positivism and the re-opening of discussion of virtually all the traditional problems of philosophy'.[47] While we may never know whether God became a live issue for Ayer before his death, the demise of positivism meant that questions of metaphysics, including the existence of God, were once again live issues in the world of academia.

Recommended Reading

Note: Material which is listed in the footnotes has not been re-listed here.

Ayer, A.J., *Language, Truth and Logic* (Penguin, 2001)
Ayer, A.J., 'What I Saw When I Was Dead' in Miethe, Terry and Flew, Antony, *Does God Exist? A Believer and an Atheist Debate* (Harper Collins, 1991)
Ayer, A.J., 'A.J. Ayer to Harrod, 2 December 1933' (letter from Ayer) – economia.unipv.it/harrod/edition/editionstuff/rfh.166.htm
Ayer, A.J., 'Language, Truth, Logic and God' (an excerpt from *Language, Truth and Logic*) – www.stephenjaygould.org/ctrl/ayer_metaphysics.html

Faithnet, 'Logical Positivism: An Introduction' – www.
faithnet.org.uk/Philosophy/logicalpositivism.htm
Magee, Bryan, 'The appeal of logical positivism' – www.
basicincome.com/bp/ratherlike.htm
Wikipedia, 'Logical Positivism' – www.wikipedia.org/
wiki/Logical_positivism

Notes

[1] Kelly James Clark, 'Introduction: The Literature of Confession', *Philosophers Who Believe* – www.calvin.edu/academic/philosophy/writings/pwbintro.htm
[2] Clark, 'Introduction'
[3] Clark, 'Introduction'
[4] Wikipedia, 'Alfred Ayer' – www.wikipedia.org/wiki/Alfred_Ayer
[5] A.J. Ayer, *Language, Truth and Logic*, 2nd edition, (Victor Gollancz, 1946), p. 115
[6] Ayer, *Language, Truth and Logic*, p. 175
[7] A.J. Ayer, *The Central Questions of Philosophy* (Penguin, 1973), p. 118–119
[8] F.C. Copleston, *Contemporary Philosophy* (Burns & Oates, 1957), p. 9
[9] Cash, William, 'Did atheist philosopher see God when he "died"?' *National Post,* 3 March 2001 – www.gonsalves.org/favorite/atheist.htm
[10] Hilary Spurling, 'The Wickedest Man in Oxford', *New York Times*, 24 December 2000 – www.nytimes.com/books/00/12/24/reviews/001224.24spurlit.html
[11] E.L. Mascall, *He Who Is* (Longmans, Green and Co., 1954), p. xi
[12] Copleston, *Contemporary Philosophy*
[13] John Hick, 'Theology and Verification' in Basil Mitchell (ed.), *The Philosophy of Religion* (Oxford, 1971), p. 69
[14] For more information, see Douglas Scott and Martin White, 'The Cosmic Microwave Background' – www.astro.ubc.ca/people/scott/cmb_intro.html

[15] Hick, 'Theology and Verification', p. 71

[16] 'According to Newton's law of gravitation, the more distant a star is from the centre of a spiral galaxy, the lower its orbiting velocity. However, observations showed that even stars in the far periphery of a galaxy orbited at nearly the same speed as those closer to the centre. To our eyes, galactic mass appears concentrated towards the centre and diminishes towards the periphery. And yet the stars at the periphery move as if they are embedded in much greater mass ... The unseen matter, by inference, must be a major component of galaxies. This came to be known as "dark matter". This non-luminous matter has not been confirmed by observations at any electromagnetic wavelength and constitutes at least 90 percent of the universe.' (Singapore Science Centre – www.science.edu.sg/ssc/detailed.jsp?artid=4191&type=6&root=6&parent=6&cat=65)

[17] Lloyd Eby, 'Viewpoint: What is Science? Part I', *World Peace Herald*, 16 December 2005 – www.wpherald.com/storyview.php?StoryID=20051216-041328-8321r

[18] For more on this, see Richard Swinburne, 'The Justification of Theism', *Truth Journal* – www.leaderu.com/truth/3truth09.html

[19] Basil Mitchell, 'Reflections on C.S. Lewis, Apologetics, and the Moral Tradition: Basil Mitchell in Conversation with Andrew Walker', in Andrew Walker and James Patrick (eds.), *Rumours of Heaven: Essays in Celebration of C.S. Lewis* (Eagle, 1998), p. 19

[20] Victor Reppert, *C.S. Lewis's Dangerous Idea* (IVP, 2003), p. 20

[21] F.C. Copleston, 'Logical Positivism – A Debate' in Paul Edwards and Arthur Pap (eds.) *A Modern Introduction to Philosophy* (The Free Press, 1965), p. 756

[22] R. Douglas Geivett, 'The Evidential Value of Religious Experience' in Paul Copan and Paul K. Moser (eds.), *The Rationality of Theism* (Routledge, 2003), p. 175

[23] William P. Alston, 'Religious Language and Verificationism' in Copan and Moser, *The Rationality of Theism*, p. 21 (author's italics)

[24] Roger Scruton, *An Intelligent Person's Guide To Philosophy* (Duckworth, 1997), p. 18

[25] Copleston, 'Logical Positivism – A Debate', p. 756

[26] Ayer, *The Central Questions of Philosophy*, p. 34

[27] Keith Ward, *God: A Guide for the Perplexed* (OneWorld, 2002), p. 184

[28] Clark, 'Introduction'

[29] William Lane Craig, 'Advice to Christian Apologists' – www.euroleadershipresources.org/resource.php?ID=99

[30] Ronald H. Nash, *Faith and Reason* (Zondervan, 1988), p. 53

[31] A.J. Ayer, quoted by Keith Ward, *The Turn of the Tide* (BBC Publications, 1986), p. 59

[32] Ayer, *The Central Questions of Philosophy*, p. 22–34

[33] A.J. Ayer, *The Listener*, 2 March 1978

[34] A.J. Ayer in Roy Abraham Vargese (ed.), *Great Thinkers on Great Questions* (OneWorld, 1998), p. 49

[35] Wikipedia, 'Alfred Ayer'

[36] Cash, 'Did atheist philosopher see God when he "died"?'

[37] For more on this, see A.J. Ayer, 'The Brains Trust' (extract from A.J. Ayer, *More of My Life* (Oxford University Press, 1984)) – atschool.eduweb.co.uk/stevemoss/bron/ayer.htm

[38] Wikipedia, 'Alfred Ayer'

[39] Cash, 'Did atheist philosopher see God when he "died"?'

[40] Cash, 'Did atheist philosopher see God when he "died"?'

[41] Cash, 'Did atheist philosopher see God when he "died"?'

[42] Cash, 'Did atheist philosopher see God when he "died"?'

[43] Cash, 'Did atheist philosopher see God when he "died"?'

[44] Cash, 'Did atheist philosopher see God when he "died"?'

[45] William Lane Craig, *Philosophy of Religion: A Reader and Guide* (Edinburgh University Press, 2001), p. 1

[46] 'Modernizing the Case for God', *Time Magazine*, 7 April 1980, pp. 65–66

[47] Tyler Burge, 'Philosophy of Language and Mind', *Philosophical Review* 101 (1992), p. 49

Background to the Featured Quotes

I'm a rational person . . . (p. xvii)

> I'm a rational person. I believe in science. I don't believe in the paranormal and I don't believe in ghosts.
>
> Dr Miranda Grey in the film *Gothika*

Source

Gothika (dir. Mathieu Kassovitz, Warner Brothers, 2003), certificate 15

Background

Gothika is the story of Miranda Grey (Halle Berry), a psychiatric doctor in an American penitentiary. One day, she wakes up to discover that she is suspected of murdering her own husband, and is now being treated at the penitentiary in which she previously worked.

Although Dr Grey does not believe in the paranormal, the scene goes on to show her saying that, if there really is a particular ghost in the cell with her, the ghost should prove it by opening the high-security door. Immediately, the door unlocks and swings open.

I couldn't let go of my faith . . . (p. 15)

I couldn't let go of my faith. But what is more interesting is that I don't think God will let go of me.

Bono

Source

'The Q Interview', *Q* magazine, January 2006, p. 66

Background

Bono is the lead singer of U2, who have arguably been the biggest rock band in the world for several years. They have a reputation for continuing to develop musically, rather than simply churn out more of the same, and their songs contain a wealth of ideas and concepts ranging from social justice and politics to spirituality and personal themes. Three of the band, including Bono, professed a Christian faith in the early days of their career, but are now wary of being closely identified with organised religion.

This quote comes as part of Bono's answer to the question: 'Money. Irishness. God. Which one couldn't you live without?' In answering, Bono recalls calling out to God in the midst of his confusion and lack of purpose following the death of his mother when he was fourteen. His sense of God's direction for his life in the following months is cited as part of the reason why he couldn't let go of his faith.

Something that looks like a miracle . . . (p. 33)

Something that looks like a miracle turns out to be dead simple.

Saint Peter in the film *Millions*

Source

Millions (dir. Danny Boyle, Pathe, 2005), certificate 12

Background

Millions tells the story of two boys who find £250,000 just a few days before sterling currency becomes worthless when Britain converts to the Euro. Damien (Alex Etal) wants to use the money to help the poor, but his older brother Anthony wants to use it to buy things and to gain influence at school.

Damien, still grieving after the recent death of the boys' mother, has become obsessed with a book of saints, and frequently has visions where he talks to the saints that he has been reading about. Damien talks with Saint Peter, who explains that the 'miracle' of feeding the 5000 was that Jesus' actions prompted everyone to start sharing the food that they had brought with them, rather than any supernatural increase in the amount of food.

However you define God ... (p. 47)

However you define God, and whether you believe in God or not, the world that we live in has been shaped by the universal human conviction that there is more to life than life itself; that there is a God-shaped hole at the centre of our universe.

Professor Robert Winston

Source

The Story of God – episode one (BBC One, 4 December 2005)

Background

Lord Robert Winston has become one of the best known faces in the world of science on British television. He is a specialist in human fertility research and presented the television series *The Human Body* and *Child of our Time* (following the development of a group of children born in 2000). He is also the presenter of *The Story of God*, a three-part documentary exploring humanity's quest to understand the nature of God. Part one, 'Life, the Universe and Everything', concerned polytheistic religions; part two, 'No God But God', focused on the great monotheistic religions; while part three, 'The God of the Gaps', explored how religion has been challenged by secular ideas, particularly science. This quote comes from the introductory remarks to the first episode.

It's natural, even healthy . . . (p. 63)

It's natural, even healthy, to question the world we're presented. You might say it's only human.

Dr Merrick in the film *The Island*

Source

The Island (dir. Michael Bay, Warner Brothers, 2005), certificate 12

Background

The Island is a science fiction thriller starring Ewan McGregor and Scarlett Johansson as two inhabitants of a high-tech medical complex. They discover that they are clones who are being kept as an 'insurance policy' for wealthy customers who want to ensure the existence of suitable donor organs in the event of illness or injury. Lincoln Six Echo (McGregor) and Jordan Two Delta (Johansson) escape, and set out to meet their counterparts in the outside world.

This quote comes when Dr Merrick (Sean Bean), the scientist who runs the cloning programme, is talking about the problems caused by Lincoln Six Echo's tendency to question both the false history he has been programmed with and also the daily environment within the complex. All of the clones are conditioned to believe that they are survivors of an environmental catastrophe, whose only hope is to win the lottery and get a place on 'the Island' – the last pathogen-free zone on Earth. In fact, when someone wins the lottery, it means that a customer has need for one or more organs and is calling in his insurance, resulting in the death of the 'lucky' clone.

Whether it's religion or my own scepticism . . . (p. 83)

Whether it's religion or my own scepticism, we all notice what supports our beliefs and we disregard the rest.
Derren Brown in *Messiah*

Source

Messiah (Channel 4, 7 January 2005)

Background

Derren Brown appears on stage and television, using his skills in 'magic, suggestion, psychology, misdirection and showmanship' to entertain and to challenge assumptions and beliefs about the supernatural. His previous TV exploits have included faking a séance and, apparently, playing Russian Roulette on live TV.

As a student, Derren Brown was a member of Christian groups (something he refers to in passing in *Messiah)*, but lost his faith when he started questioning the things he believed and found that his leaders were not comfortable with the questions he was asking. Brown's main purpose in *Messiah* seems to be to encourage people to question, rather than taking major life decisions on trust.

In *Messiah*, Brown travels around America (where he is unknown) and attempts to convince respected authority figures from five very different belief systems to endorse him as a gifted practitioner of the things they believe in.

Hell is waking up ... (p. 101)

Hell is waking up every Goddamn day and not even knowing why you're here.

Marv in the film *Sin City*

Source

Sin City (dir. Frank Miller, Dimension, 2005), certificate 18

Background

Sin City is a violent, bloody cinematic version of Frank Miller's graphic novels of the same name. It is a brutal, disturbing noir-styled thriller, made up of a number of interlocking storylines drawn from the archives of the original comic books.

Marv (Mickey Rourke) is an ex-convict who has been set up and framed for somebody else's murder. His parole officer reminds him that his last prison sentence was 'hell for you', and warns that this time he can expect a life sentence. The quote is Marv's response.

It doesn't always make sense . . . (p. 111)

It doesn't always make sense, and most of it never happened. But that's the kind of story this is.
Ed Bloom in the film Big Fish

Source

Big Fish (dir. Tim Burton, Columbia TriStar, 2003), certificate PG

Background

Big Fish tells the story of Edward Bloom (played at different stages of his life by a number of actors, primarily Ewan McGregor and Albert Finney) and his son William. Ed has always told fantastic stories about his life, much to the frustration of William, who longs to know the real truth about his father's life.

I think to believe in life after death . . . (p. 121)

I think to believe in life after death you would have to believe in God, and if I believed in God I would have to forgo a lot of my other rational and scientific beliefs.

It would mean a complete restructuring of the way I see the world.

Simon Armitage

Source

Simon Jones, 'Style Counsel', *Third Way* magazine, November 2005, p. 17

Background

Simon Armitage is a successful and award winning poet who has been published since 1989. His books include *Book of Matches* (Faber & Faber, 2001), *Travelling Songs* (Faber & Faber, 2002), *Short and Sweet: 101 Very Short Poems* (Faber & Faber, 2002). As well as poetry, he has also written for stage, radio, television and film.

This quote comes as Armitage's response to being asked what he meant when he once said that life after death is 'a great offer, but the price is too high'.

For Further Reading

Paul Copan and Paul K. Moser (eds.), *The Rationality of Theism* (Routledge, 2003)

William Lane Craig, *Philosophy of Religion: A Reader and Guide* (Edinburgh University Press, 2001)

Sydney H.T. Page, *Powers of Evil: A Biblical Study of Satan and Demons* (IVP, 1995)

Victor Reppert, *C.S. Lewis's Dangerous Idea* (IVP, 2003)

Nigel Wright, *The Fair Face of Evil: Putting the Power of Darkness in Its Place* (Marshall Pickering, 1989)

Other titles in the *Talking About* series

Sex and the Cynics: Talking About the Search for Love

Truth Wars: Talking About Tolerance

Playing God: Talking About Ethics in Medicine and Technology

Other titles from Damaris Books

Get More Like Jesus While Watching TV
by Nick Pollard and Steve Couch

Teenagers: Why Do They Do That?
by Nick Pollard

Saving Sex: Answers to Teenagers' Questions About Relationships and Sex (due for publication Spring 2006)
by Dr Trevor Stammers and Tim Doak

Back In Time: A thinking fan's guide to Doctor Who
by Steve Couch, Tony Watkins and Peter S. Williams

Dark Matter: A thinking fan's guide to Philip Pullman
by Tony Watkins

Matrix Revelations: A thinking fan's guide to the Matrix trilogy
edited by Steve Couch

I Wish I Could Believe In Meaning
by Peter S. Williams

If Only
by Nick Pollard

CultureWatch
(free access website)

CultureWatch explores the message behind the media through hundreds of articles and study guides on films, books, music and television. It is written from a distinctively Christian angle, but is appropriate for people of all faiths and people of no faith at all.

CULTUREWATCH
http://www.damaris.org/cw